RACING TOWARD...

THE MARK OF THE BEAST

PETER LALONDE & PAUL LALONDE

HARVEST HOUSE PUBLISHERS
Eugene, Oregon 97402

Scripture quotations in this book are taken from the King James Version of the Bible.

THE MARK OF THE BEAST

Copyright © 1994 by Harvest House Publishers
Eugene, Oregon 97402

Library of Congress Cataloging-in-Publication Data

Lalonde, Peter.
  The mark of the beast / Peter Lalonde, Paul Lalonde.
    p.   cm.
  ISBN 1-56507-218-9
  1. Bible—Prophecies—International organization.
  2. Beast of the Apocalypse. 3. Bible—Prophecies—Armageddon.
  4. Bible. N.T. Revelation XIII, 16-17—Criticism, interpretation, etc.
  5. Bible—Prophecies—Communication—International cooperation.
  I. Lalonde, Paul. II. Title.
  BS649.I56L335 1994
  236'.9—dc20   93-43734
                                                                CIP

Printed in the United States of America.

Contents

1

Boy, Have I Got Your Number

Myles first saw her driving her jet-black BMW 520i convertible during the morning rush hour. Traffic was actually moving quickly enough for her shiny black hair to dance in the breeze. She was stunning, and Myles knew he had to find out more about this beauty. He slowed slightly so that he could read her license plate. It read simply, MY TOY.

Myles drove directly to his office building and rushed through the lobby. *Why does the elevator always stop at every floor when you're in a hurry?* Myles thought as he stared at the numbers above the door. Finally, the bell rang and the doors slid open.

"Good morning, Mr. Thompson," said the pretty receptionist.

"Good morning, Janice." Myles obviously was distracted. "Do I have any messages?"

"Just Mrs. Wilson—she still can't get Dennis to stop swearing at his teachers." Myles loved his job as a social worker, and was actually quite involved in the Wilson case. But for now, he hardly heard Janice's words.

Inside his office, Myles sat down at his desk, flipped on the power switch to his computer, and drummed his fingers on the desk while the machine booted up. A few beeps from the speaker signaled that he was ready to begin. He entered his password: L-O-N-E-L-Y. The computer answered him on the screen, *"Good morning, Myles."*

He browsed through the seemingly endless options and finally found it.

Press 345 to access the
Department of Motor Vehicles.

Myles keyed in the numbers and then typed in the only information he had . . . and the only information he needed.

License Number:
MY TOY, California

"Please wait" sat on his screen forever. Finally, Myles hit pay dirt.

License: MY TOY
Registration: California
Vehicle: 1994 BMW 520i Sedan

Registered to: Kathi Lee Simpson
4565 Cedar Line Rd.
Venice, CA
Driver's License #: 3453-9987-0987
Date of Birth: 08-25-61
Sex: Female
Height: 5'7"
Weight: 112 lbs.

As a social worker, Myles did a lot of investigations, trying to find information on the families he worked with. From experience, he knew that the number on Kathi's driver's license was also her social security number. With that number, he also was confident in the fact that he had found the key to the personal life of this black-haired beauty. Myles never for one second considered that what he was doing might be wrong. It was just the way of the world of the nineties worked.

He worked the keyboard like a seasoned professional. First he accessed the database that kept the records that employers must file with the state unemployment compensation and tax offices. Bingo!

Employer: Foster, Kleiner and
Brown Advertising
Position: Vice-President
Gross Pay 1993: $88,402
First Quarter Earnings 1994: $37,500

Myles knew that Kathi must just have been promoted. Based on her first quarter earnings,

Kathi was now at a wage of $150,000. *Not bad*, he thought.

Next Myles accessed the database at the Register's Office where local deeds were filed. He typed in Kathi's address and *presto!*

> *Address: 8429 Executive Way,*
> *Block 103, Lot 2*
> *Land Assessed: $41,202*
> *Improved Assessment: $83,602*
> *Total Assessment: $124,804*
> *Built: 1990*
> *Use: Residential*
> *Deed of Trust Recorded: 11/3/90*
> *Loan Instrument: 23489*
> *Amount: $93,603*
> *Mortgage Info: Mortgage Between*
> *Alex and Kathi Lee Brown*
> *and First National Bank*

Wait a minute, Myles thought. Kathi's name was Kathi Lee Simpson, not Kathi Lee Brown. Who was this Alex character? Myles accessed the county divorce records and found his answer.

> *Divorce: 5/7/92*
> *Case: Kathi Lee Brown vs. Alex Brown*
> *Married: 2/14/80*
> *Children: (2) Jonathan (born 2/7/81);*
> *Marie (born 4/6/83)*
> *Grounds: Infidelity*
> *Previous Marriages: Husband (1); Wife (0)*

Myles knew that he had seen all he needed here. The next step, as always, was the children. Myles knew from experience that the way to Kathi's heart would be through her children. The school enrollment records were easy to find and gave Myles some valuable information to use in his first contact with Kathi. Jonathan was 13 years old, an above average student, and a member of the three school baseball teams. That little piece of information would be Myles's foot in the door.

But Myles was determined to be completely prepared when he met this lady who only grew in beauty each time he thought of her. He didn't want to blow this, so he had to have more information. Despite Myles's access to all kinds of classified databases, he was not allowed to access the IRS files directly. However, a list was mailed by the state welfare office where he worked to the IRS each day. By putting Kathi's name on this list, he could get tax information about her unearned income. A couple of days later the data had arrived:

> *Form 1090—Unearned Income. Interest: $1,500 from $25,000 CD at First National, $3,200 from $50,000 CD at Upper Valley Savings and Loan; Dividends: $2,600 Lawrence Furniture, $14,000 sales of Microsoft stock; Other: $7,500 rental of house at 2250 Yonge Street, $2,850 winning from wagers at Highland Race Track.*

Myles reflected on what he had learned. Kathi was very well off financially and successful in her business. She filed for divorce after charging her husband with adultery. She owned two homes, a luxury car, and had custody of her two children. Her son loved baseball and Kathi loved to play the ponies. That was a good enough start.

Before he knew it, it was after 7 P.M. and Myles was ready. He reached for the phone, took a deep breath, and dialed the number.

"Hello?" It was a woman's voice.

"Hello, Ms. Simpson?"

"Yes—who is this?"

"My name is Myles Thompson, and I hope you won't think me too forward, but I feel as if I already know you."

"What do you mean?" Kathi asked.

"I was at a reception last night here in the city and I was talking to a fellow who works in the advertising business. We talked for a long time and he told me about you. He also told me all about your son, Jonathan, and how much he loves baseball." Myles was studying the papers on his desk as he spoke, making sure that he didn't make any mistakes. "He told me about your divorce and said that he thought you and I had much in common. And it just so happens that I have some good friends with the California Angels baseball team, and when I mentioned that I could get Jonathan some great autographs, this guy suggested that I call you. I thought maybe you and Jonathan would like to go sometime." By this time, Myles's hands were soaked with sweat and his hands trembled slightly. But his voice was clear and confident—and for now, that was all that mattered.

"Gee, who was it you were talking to?" Kathi inquired. Here was where the rubber hit the road. This had to be handled perfectly.

"This is really embarrassing," Myles said, "but I honestly can't remember this guy's name. He was a tall fellow, mid-thirties, but I'm just not very good with names. All I know is that he is in advertising."

"Oh, it must be one of the men at my agency— I'm in advertising, too," Kathi said. "I know that Jonathan would be very excited about the autographs. Why don't we try for the game against the Blue Jays next week?"

"That would be great," Myles replied. He couldn't believe how easy this was. "Oh, there's just one thing, though—would you mind if I stopped on the way for a few minutes at Highland Race Track? There are just a few small wagers I'd like to make."

Reality Is Stranger Than Fiction

Of course, this is a fictional story designed to give you an idea of the kind of data that is easily accessible about all of us. But far from being an overstated example, this story is a good deal less alarming than what can and does take place in our world every day. In fact, Democrat Bob Wise of West Virginia, who heads the House Subcommittee on the government's use of databases, has reached the conclusion that "in the not too distant future, consumers face the prospect that a computer somewhere will compile records about every place they go and everything they purchase."[1]

In the not too distant future, consumers face the prospect that a computer somewhere will compile records about every place they go and everything they purchase.

David Linowes, the former chairman of the U.S. Privacy Protection Commission, also is worried:

> The danger is not that direct marketing companies will clog your mailbox or call you during dinner to hawk commemorative coins. The danger is that employers, banks and government agencies will use databases to make decisions about our lives without our knowing about it.[2]

A De Facto National Data Bank

Recently, a study for Congress by the Office of Technology Assessment pointed out that advances in supercomputer databases have actually created a de facto national database "containing substantial personal information about most Americans."

But rather than being an Orwellian central data bank that maintains records in one place—something like the National Data Center that was rejected by Congress more than a decade ago—this "de facto national database" is created from hundreds of separate computerized record systems that can be reached over telephone lines by computers from virtually anywhere in the country. By searching out information on an individual through a variety of these computerized data banks, the study noted, it is possible today for government officials to compile electronic dossiers on millions of private citizens.

It is possible today to electronically mingle, merge, and compare three billion records containing personal information held by various federal agencies alone. The system has become so extensive, the report said, that it is difficult for individuals to know what files about them exist, whether the information contained in those files is accurate, and whether any information they may have supplied voluntarily to one agency for one purpose is being used by another agency for another purpose.

Jerry Bergman, director of the American Civil Liberty Union's privacy and technology project, said:

> If Congress tried to introduce a bill to establish a central file on every citizen, it would go down to defeat, but this report shows that what couldn't be done frontally has happened incrementally.[3]

In Canada the situation is no better. Gerry Montigny, an information specialist in the federal Privacy Commissioner's Office, sees the trend going global:

We're headed for a world where there is basically one computer with a whole bunch of links. In theory, any computer can talk to any other computer.[4]

President Clinton's Smart Idea

If you are going to have a system that contains this kind of information, then you must be certain that the right files are cross-referenced with the right files. The only way to do this logically is to make sure every single person in the system has a unique and personal number. Names are too common and confusing. Only numbers are truly unique.

Every child would be numbered at birth, put into a national database, and tracked for life.

So how far have we come in this new information age? How close are we to the day when we become the numbered and tracked society foreseen by George Orwell and Aldous Huxley? The Clinton administration provides one clue. Clinton is advocating the use of "smart cards" tied to Social Security account numbers to provide every citizen of the country with a universal identity card. In order to be covered by the national health care system, participation in the national identity program will be mandatory. Under the Clinton proposal, every child would be numbered at birth, put into a national database, and tracked for life. Children would be required by law to participate in vaccination and public health programs. Failure by parents to fulfill state-mandated medical decisions would be evidence of child abuse and the children could be placed in foster care.

The current U.S. administration is putting huge effort into a de facto national ID card. President Clinton has gone so far as to say that regardless of any other disagreements, all members of Congress should unite behind this single goal!

National Notary magazine has announced that Clinton's idea is a notion whose time has come:

> It's not very often that a Democrat and a Republican agree, but President Bill Clinton and California Governor Pete Wilson appear to be on the same wavelength about the need for a national identification card.

> Clinton is suggesting a computer readable identification card as part of his proposed national health plan and Wilson is advocating a citizen ID to help stem the tide of illegal aliens. . . .

> Recently U.S. Attorney General Janet Reno toured the U.S.-Mexican border and was shown more than 200 fake identification cards typical of those used by illegal immigrants and drug smugglers.

INS border patrol agents told Reno they seize 100-200 such false identifications each weekend.[5]

National Card Sets National Agenda

The truth probably is that there is no escaping the system. In June 1986 the Supreme Court ruled that the government may force citizens to have a Social Security card. The case arose when a native American claimed that "numbers and computers used to identify people are part of a great evil." The Court ruled that freedom of religion "does not afford an individual the right to dictate the conduct of the government's internal procedures."

Moreover, based on the 1983 Immigration Reform and Control Act, employers would have to obtain documents proving the citizenship or immigration status of all new employees within 24 hours of hiring them.

This can only mean that all Americans could be forced to show acceptable government identification when applying for jobs in the future. Since ordinary ID is easy to forge or obtain illegally, the cry will soon go up for a national ID card for each American.

Once such a card is issued, it is only a matter of time until Americans must have that government ID card in their possession at all times, and the command of modern tyrants will be heard on our own soil: "Show me your papers!"[6]

When you consider that Social Security numbers are being given to toddlers, presumably too young to go out and get a full-time job, the idea that a system of national identification is being born is not so outlandish—and the potential for its misuse is great. Here's what the *Communicator*, a publication of the Smart Card Industry Association, says:

> The average American already carries a Social Security card by age one, a driver's license by age 18, a health card by age 22, a passport if you want to leave the country, a voter's registration card, a membership card of some type, some kind of emergency medical treatment card, an ATM card, a phone card, and a car insurance card. Almost all of this information is filed with the government or can be accessed by some government agency now.... In theory, if all of these groups got together to develop one universal system, with varying levels of security, you could put all of this information on one smart card.... A cradle to the grave medical smart card is an excellent idea![7]

Don't Let It Get Under Your Skin

Martin Anderson, writing in the *Washington Times*, points out a problem that is central to this brave new world. He says that this national ID card will become so necessary in order "to comply with government regulations" that people will be forced to carry it with them "at all times."[8] Moreover, the question is, What happens if we lose our card or it is stolen? Could someone else use it and pretend to be us?

Anderson, a senior fellow at the Hoover Institution and a syndicated columnist, points out that much thought is going into this very problem:

> You see, there is an identification system made by the Hughes Aircraft Company that you can't lose. It's a syringe implantable transponder. According to promotional literature, it is an "ingenious, safe, inexpensive, foolproof and permanent method of . . . identification using radio waves. A tiny microchip, the size of a grain of rice, is simply placed under the skin. It is so designed as to be injected simultaneously with a vaccination or alone. . . ."
>
> Of course, most Americans will find a surgically implanted government microchip repugnant. At least for the foreseeable future, the use of this ingenious device will be confined to its current use: the tracking of dogs, cats, horses and cattle.
>
> But there is no difference in principle between being forced to carry a microchip in a plastic card in your wallet or in a little pellet in your arm. The principle that Big Brother has the right to track you is inherent in both. The only thing that differentiates the two techniques is a layer of skin.[9]

Excuse Me, Sir, I've Heard That Somewhere Before!

As incredible as all of these technological advances are, and as thought-provoking as they may be to those who have read about "Big Brother," there is something much, much more stunning to be noticed here. You see, the Bible predicted just such a system more than 2,000 years ago! And it wasn't in some strange symbolism or allegoric language that you'd need three Ph.D.s and half a dozen computers to figure out, either:

> And he [the false prophet, working under the antichrist] causeth all, both small and great, rich and poor, free and bond, to receive a mark in their right hand, or in their foreheads: And that no man might buy or sell, save he that had the mark, or the name of the beast . . . for it is the number of a man; and his number is Six hundred threescore and six (Revelation 13:16,17).

Think about what this text is saying. The Bible is telling us that under this "666 system" no one on earth will be allowed to buy or sell anything unless he or she receives a mark in the forehead or right hand. This simplicity, combined with the powerful technological developments which are doubtless necessary to fulfill these words—words penned in the age of wood, stones, and the toga—make this prophecy one of the most powerful proofs of the accuracy of God's Word. Indeed, the prophecy itself contains only 63 words, yet it will take the entirety of this book to document how precisely those words have foreshadowed the modern-day, computerized, global economic structure.

No one can say precisely what technology will ultimately be used to fulfill the prophecy of the mark of the beast, but this book is designed to explore the possibilities and the advances in technology that make such a universal system possible. But one thing is certain: By the time you have read this book, you'll be more amazed at the power of God than with the power of any of the incredible, space-age technologies we will talk about.

We guarantee it.

2

Kiss Your Cash Goodbye

Imagine walking into a grocery store and buying all of your weekly groceries without ever needing money, your credit cards, or a check. Imagine having the funds you need for your purchases magically transferred directly from your checking account into the store's bank account.

This is the heart of the cashless world that planners have been predicting for years. Through the use of debit cards, they say, we can enter a brave new world where every transaction, every purchase, and every sale can be conducted electronically.

When we first began to report on the emergence of the technology that could bring the cashless society into being, many people thought we were a little paranoid. Some didn't even know what we were talking about because they were from small towns or rural areas where the technology hadn't yet made a major appearance. They thought we had gone off the deep end!

They can't say that anymore (at least for those reasons). Today, we are witnessing the birth of an electronic world—a world of fax machines, personal computers, Nintendo games, and, of course, automated banking machines which tell us in a matter of seconds if our credit cards have been pushed to the limit once again.

The cashless world is not quite here, but there are few people who doubt we've finally stepped onto the fast track. Just last November we were flying to our annual West Coast Bible Prophecy Conference in Los Angeles. On that flight we were working on this book when the television monitor came on with a news program featuring the coming cashless society. It was as if the Lord was reminding us how quickly things were happening.

We watched with interest how this report so casually stated that the world of electronic banking was here and that, except for a few novel uses, cash was on its way out. We looked around the aircraft and saw our thinking of the past few months confirmed. *No one cared*. No one paid any special attention to the details of the report; no one nudged the person in the next seat to take a look. The "news" doesn't surprise anyone.

The report noted the eagerness with which people are ready to embrace a cashless world. It stated that a recent Gallup poll in the United States showed that 64 percent of people polled would approve a system that is more convenient than the current cash-and-check world in which we live. Sixty-six percent said that cash is too easy to lose or have stolen. Forty-eight percent called checks too slow and inconvenient. And 23 percent within the last 12 months have had the unpleasant experience of getting to the checkout counter without enough money.[1]

If the antichrist is to have control of every sale or purchase, it appears that cash must be eliminated so that there will be a record of every transaction.

This is extremely good news to the cashless world's leading architects. Why? Because their brainchild has been moving at a snail's pace in the last 15 or so years, especially in Canada and the United States. Public resistance to cashlessness, rather than delays in technology, explains the slow trend. The public has read George Orwell's *1984* and Aldous Huxley's *Brave New World*, with their nightmarish visions of the future, and has resisted the technology and has been leery of the possibilities implicit in such a system. Still, recent polls suggest that the consumer's slow acceptance is a thing of the past. Meanwhile, technological advances have continued at a staggering rate.

A Cashless Society at the Heart of the Beast System

To reiterate a critical matter: It seems to us that a cashless society is crucial to the prophesied mark-of-the-beast system. The Scripture says:

> That no man might buy or sell, save he that had the mark, or the name of the beast, or the number of his name (Revelation 13:17).

If the antichrist is to have control of every sale or purchase, it appears that cash must be eliminated so that there will be a record of every transaction. If cash were permitted in the coming new world order, some commercial activities could be accomplished outside the system. The antichrist could not control the buying power of every citizen if even a few deals were closed with cash.

Printed documentation is too bulky and slow, so an elaborate and sophisticated electronic system that controls and documents every transaction must almost certainly be in place. It must be a universal system since it will control every transaction of every person everywhere. Thus, the worldwide use of plastic cards today is only a natural and necessary step to a cashless society.

In this chapter we are going to look at the growing demand for a cashless society. Many retailers, bankers, governments, law enforcement agencies, and even ordinary citizens are beginning to demand a change from our present way of conducting business. The outcries for change are beginning to drown out the voice of resistance—and those with the vision and technology are waiting in the wings, ready to respond immediately when public demand reaches the necessary crescendo.

The Choice of a New Generation

Perhaps the main resistance has come from what we'll call the over-45 crowd. Most people in this age group have struggled with the computer age—not because of their age, but because they're not comfortable with the technology. This generation prefers human and personal contact and does most of its personal banking at the teller counter inside the bank. Its members are more comfortable with human contact than with using the drive-through window or an automated teller machine.

The situation reminds us of the wallpaper hanging in one of our homes. The wallpaper features newspaper ads for late 1800-era Toronto businesses. One ad asks consumers, "Do you know how important light is to your health?" The ad was trying to convince consumers to turn in their candles for electric lights. How far we've come! In our generation, it's a real adventure trying to figure out how to get ready for school or work when the power goes out.

This small example illustrates how change is difficult for every generation. We remember when

Canada converted to the metric system. It happened more than 20 years ago when we were not yet teenagers, but we still measure in feet and inches and relate better to 80 degrees Fahrenheit than we do to 27 degrees Celsius—even though they are the same thing!

But back to the discussion. Men and women in this 45-and-older category struggle with the dramatic changes hitting the scene. Only a few in this generation are daring enough to try an ATM. I know of one woman who believed if she hit a wrong key, she could foul up the computer in the Pentagon or the Kremlin and begin a nuclear war! Most of this age group are not familiar with simple computer functions. Terms such as *megabyte*, *software*, *hardware*, and *RAM* are a foreign language to them—and like all humans, they are afraid of unfamiliar things they don't understand.

Fear of computers, combined with the impersonal business transactions and "techy" lingo, have helped to keep many citizens in the "cash is best" mindset. Prove it to yourself by visiting a bank. Inside you'll see mainly older people lined up at the teller windows. Then look outside. You'll see mainly younger people lined up at the ATMs.

Slowly, however, even this older group is beginning to change. The culture shock of the computer age is beginning to wear off. Little by little they are realizing that ATMs are not envoys of the devil; they can't cause a worldwide disaster (or even a local one) if a wrong number is punched in.

As more seniors are traveling in their retirement, they realize the necessity of having a credit card to rent a car, make purchases or phone calls, or check into most hotels. Seniors are realizing that plastic money is safer than carrying large amounts of cash when they travel—especially to areas where tourists have become prime marks for criminals.

Without meaning to sound crass or callous, there is another factor in the decreasing popularity of cash. The older holdouts are dying off. Their opposition will be eliminated either by attrition or by economic necessity when they become a very small minority.

ATMs: Tellers Without the Attitudes

As the over-45 crowd is beginning to relax with today's technology, the under-45 crowd is passionately embracing it. The younger group prefers the speed and ease of dealing with an electronic teller. These young people are a product of the computer age. They're more accustomed to interacting with machines than they are with humans. Think of the hours spent with computer games, video machines, and home computers. It would only make sense that banking with a machine would appeal to them.

In a "man-on-the-street" segment for our "This Week in Bible Prophecy" program, we found that people under 45 years old overwhelmingly preferred dealing with a nonhuman teller. The most common reason cited by the younger set was the convenience of banking at any hour. Several people commented that ATMs rarely have long lines, and one young man offered this reason: "Automated teller machines are not moody."

Whatever the reasons, more and more people are finding electronic banking more compatible with their busier and more mobile lifestyles.

Big Brother Who?

Unlike a few years ago, our more recent research has found that the fear of Big Brother no longer plays a significant role in the resistance to a cashless society. Basically, no one is afraid of Big Brother anymore.

We surveyed people to find out whether they were concerned that governments (from municipalities to the federal level), the banking industry, and other entities have vast amounts of information about them, and that they can be tracked almost constantly by some agency or other. The younger folks (we're still using 45 years of age as the dividing line) in particular were very clear to declare their unconcern. "I have nothing to hide," they say. "The government only does this to make things more convenient and secure for us."

Since every government in history which has had this kind of information has used it in a very Big-Brother-like way, it seems to us we *should* be concerned! Look what happened in the Soviet Union when the government began to track unregistered church groups and plant KGB operatives within family units. This new generation doesn't seem to remember, understand, or care about the privacy issue and the inherent dangers of an intrusive government. They also forget that although their present leaders and the present political climate may seem nonintrusive, today's technology always falls into tomorrow's hands.

Of course, there is cause for concern. Credit card companies, banks, and government agencies have access to much information on every one of us. By pooling, combining, and cross-referencing, they can develop huge, detailed databases. We will look at all this and the possible dangers to privacy in a later chapter, but at this point it's well worth quoting our cousin who observes that "if you're not paranoid, it's because you aren't paying attention!"

In essence, fear of government control, fear of personal tracking, and fear of Big Brother have disappeared. With that is also disappearing much of the resistance to electronic commerce and a cashless society.

Like It or Not—Your Future Has Been Planned

While resistance is lessening, bankers and the card companies would still like to see the cashless society progressing much more quickly. In that light, we should realize that the cashless society is not unfolding randomly or merely because the consumer wants to take advantage of available technology. The technology is being developed at the urging of financiers because they have something to gain from a cashless system. As one banker put it, "Electronic funds transfer will come because the banks are pushing this concept forward, not because some stores just happen to be putting ATMs in their checkout lines."

At the beginning of this chapter we talked about walking into your grocery store and paying for your cheese and baloney by having the funds transferred directly from your checking account to the store's bank account. This is already being done in thousands of test locations with the use of a debit card.

What is a debit card? It looks just like a credit card but has far different capabilities. When you get to the checkout counter, you place your debit card into a point of sale (POS) terminal. The POS is linked to your bank and the store's bank. Immediately, the machine activates central computers that instantly transfer the necessary money from your account to the store's. It's all done electronically and it's about as convenient as you can get. But convenience is not the only drawing card for this new system.

Store Owners Don't Want Your Cash!

Retailers are anxious for the advent of the cashless society for a variety of profit-oriented reasons. The use of plastic debit cards translates into higher profits because of reduced employee theft (there is no cash to steal), reduced charges on noncash transactions, and the elimination of check fraud.

Moreover, preliminary studies on the use of debit cards indicate that consumers tend to spend up to three times more with a debit card than they would with a credit card. This would seem to be uncharacteristic of Western economic spending patterns, but it is nevertheless true. It seems that consumers spend more freely when they're not concerned about future payments and high interest rates.

Another plus for the retailer is the lower transaction fees charged by banks. Under the existing credit card system, retailers pay between three and seven percent of the purchase price to the credit card company. These fees, in addition to the interest charged the consumer, is how the credit card companies make their money.

The rates charged by the companies have been determined by several factors. One includes unlawful and fraudulent use of the card. Another concerns cardholders who will not or cannot pay their bills. To cover these huge losses, the companies must charge higher rates. With debit cards or prepaid cards (we'll discuss these in a moment), however, the amount of the purchase is deducted immediately from the consumer's account or card, and there is no chance that the bill will go unpaid.

Debit That Credit Card

Another consideration for the retailer is improved cash flow and more immediate access to card transaction funds. To begin with, we want to show how the elimination of cash and checks can aid the retailer and others in the money chain. There are several ways to pay for purchases at a retail outlet. The most common is to pay cash. Another common but more complex method is through personal checks.

In this payment plan, the consumer presents the store with a check for his or her purchases. At the end of the day the check is sent to a clearing-house or the store's bank, then to the consumer's bank, where the funds are debited from the account. If there are insufficient funds, then the check has to go back to the store's bank where the funds will be taken back out of the store's account. The entire process gets even more ridiculously complicated if the customer is from out of state.

A third payment method is to use a credit card. The store accepts the consumer's credit card as payment. Then the store can do one of two things. In the older, manual system a clerk or bookkeeper can write up a sales draft. At the end of the day all the handwritten drafts can be taken to the bank where they will be credited to the store's account. Or the store can electronically process the transactions. The funds will then appear in the store's account in a day or two. The information is passed along to the consumer's credit card company, which sends a bill to the consumer.

If the consumer has gone over his credit limit or the purchase is declined for any other reason, the whole transaction has to be reversed and the funds get debited again from the store's account. A lot of paperwork for a rather simple (and often small) transaction! Consider that the cardholder now pays the credit card company by check, and here we go again...

The debit card, on the other hand—which is more like cash than any other method of payment—has big advantages to the retailer. The consumer's debit card is scanned by the store clerk. Within seconds, the money is transferred directly from the consumer's account to the store's account. Or, in the case of stored-value or prepaid cards, the amount of the purchase is debited from the card on the spot. No waiting. No paperwork. No risk of NSF (non-sufficient funds) checks. It's done.

Another very important advantage for the retailer is the reduction of robbery. As fewer transactions are conducted with cash, rarely will there be large amounts of cash around the store to attract armed robbers. These reduced risks have certain obvious advantages, but there are others: reducing insurance premiums, reducing the threat of physical violence to employees and resultant medical costs. The move to cashlessness will have a chain reaction of benefits for the retailer.

On every continent, all of these advantages already have been borne out by thousands of small-scale experiments. Cashless "mini societies" have been established and have met with great success. Retailers and consumers alike said they have benefited from the cashless system.

The Cash Cards Are Coming, the Cash Cards Are Coming!

One of the big challenges cashless-society planners face is the millions of small transactions that take place every day. These can range from calls on a pay phone to bus fare to paying a parking meter. An ingenious solution has been found by combining the features of a debit card with those of something known as a prepaid card. These prepaid cards are not yet widely known in North America, but they are about to be.

A prepaid card is simply a card that has encoded within it a stored value—say, 50 local telephone calls or 20 bus trips. You buy this card at the store and each time you use it one use is deducted from the total available. When the card has been completely used, you throw it away and buy a new one.

The power of this type of card is that it does not need to access a central computer or your bank account every time you make a small purchase. As industry standards are established and the prepaid card is merged with the debit card, cash will become obsolete.

Surprise: Students Without Cash

One of the most successful transitions from cash to prepaid cards has been at the University of Rochester. It has become a cashless campus. Students, vendors, and administrators have radically changed the way they do business by using Allcard, a debit card that stores monetary value. The approval rating for the system has been very high.

The school's administration (a retailer, in this scenario) was very impressed by the program, primarily because of savings to the university. Stephen P. Klass, director of business affairs and operations for the university's services division, said, "In the past, our copying, vending and dining programs were separate revenue streams, with separate administrative personnel and accounting systems."[2]

He explained that those functions have been combined under the Allcard plan and the university has realized substantial savings.

Klass also reported that participation in on-campus dining programs increased under the new cashless system, thus increasing revenue for the university. Students use their cards at vending machines, library copiers, dorm laundries, and many other locations on campus such as the bookstore and the hair salon. After discounting increased sales due to the novelty of the system, vendors and campus shops still have consistently reported an increase of about 15 percent in business since the card system was activated.

Joe Shaw, director of operations for Anderson Paramount Food Service and Vending, which operates the campus vending machines, says of the new system:

> We're all for it. We think it's the wave of the future. We've seen a 15 percent increase in sales since the conversion. Our repair costs are lower and our accountability is better.[3]

A stylist at the campus hair salon agrees: "In a very busy week, we serve 150 to 200 students. I like the convenience [of the card system]. I'd say business is up 10 to 15 percent since we started taking the card."[4]

Kiss Your Coins Goodbye, Too

The real winner, however, is the university

itself. Ross E. McIntyre, manager of the operations and service division for the university, listed the advantages of the cashless system:

> The key is to eliminate cash points. If you have 100 machines on campus, that's 100 cash-collection points. We figure we've eliminated 5,000 to 10,000 quarters a week.

> Eliminate coins, and you cut vandalism at the machines—and make it a lot easier to secure the few cash points you still need. Also, the card reader is the most reliable mechanism for accounting for funds. It doesn't break down the way coin slides do, and it gives you a better audit trail, so you can generate better reports. You have more control with less staff time. You get out of the coin business.[5]

It's All the Card You'll Ever Need

The Rochester experiment enjoyed more success than endeavors on other campuses, and McIntyre believes he knows why. His answer holds the secret to much wider applications.

> To be successful, you need to have a large number of services on the card. Some schools start with just one service—vending machines, for example, or library copiers—and wonder why they aren't successful. That approach won't work. Users must see

the card as a convenience. You have to have a plan. You need to begin with several essential services—as we did with library copiers, vending machines, and laundries— and then add others at a reasonable pace.[6]

And what about the students? Tarra Walker, a religion major from Oregon, said, "I use my card all the time—at the laundry, the library, at vending machines. I even use it to pay for haircuts. You don't need cash when you use it, so you don't have to worry about carrying around quarters."[7]

The vast majority of Rochester's 6,000 students and 3,000 employees are regularly using their cards. And while this is an experimental program, the success of such tests boosts the confidence of pre-paid card producers. They are convinced, and have been for some time, that this is the wave of the future. They have simply been waiting for the public to catch a glimpse of this future.

Smarten Up!

Robert J. Merkert, Sr., senior vice president of Danyl Corporation of Moorestown, New Jersey (the company that developed the Allcard system for the University of Rochester), says:

> One day in the near future, we'll be able to pay for almost everything with just one "prepaid stored value" or "smart" card.[8]

Merkert, a respected proponent of cashless technology, told a gathering of business and government leaders from around the world that prepaid cards "will be used as pocket change. As prices for buses, vending machines and laundry go up, it becomes unwieldy to carry around five or ten dollars' worth of coins."[9]

Merkert also told the gathering that the transition to prepaid cards would be relatively simple. He explained that financial institutions have used credit cards for decades and ATM or debit cards for several years. As applications increase for prepaid cards, Merkert said, more banks will issue them. With universal bank-sponsored prepaid cards on the way in and coins on the way out—with no change to make and little cash around—store checkout lines will be shorter; more pay phones will be in working order; vending machine prices can increase in one-cent rather than five-cent increments; and security will be improved at laundromats, convenience stores, and gas stations.

Merkert also told the conference that each year there are more than 270 billion payment transactions in the United States alone that involve two dollars or less. He said:

> Eventually, we can install equipment that will allow users to access multiple applications with one card. When these transactions are made electronically by smart card, there will be tremendous improvement in efficiency, reduced vandalism and fewer safety problems.[10]

By having one card that essentially has two parts—the debit card function and the prepaid portion—you will ultimately have a card that can handle all transactions, both small and large. This means that a central database will have to be accessed only for larger transactions and those occasional times when the prepaid part of the card needs to be updated.

And I Like It Too!

Consumers also are beginning to see advantages to using debit/prepaid cards. Credit cards are convenient and for that reason often are overused. Inevitably, however, D day comes—the due date. Many people are surprised by how large the debt grows each month and how rapidly the minimum amount due increases. With some credit card rates exceeding 20 percent (even in this period of reduced interest rates in all other areas of the economy), the minimum payment just barely covers the monthly interest.

In Ontario, Canada, a survey of debit card users showed that 90 percent of respondents would prefer to use debit cards over credit cards. The most-often-cited reason was the reduced worry about future payments. Debit card users in London, England, reported a 97 percent approval rating for transactions and said they would continue to use the cards.[11]

When consumers can use one card for a variety of purchases, it will be more convenient for them and they will want to use the cards even more.

These point-of-sale advantages for the retailer and the consumer may not, in themselves, bring about a ground swell of support for the new money, but these positive reactions—combined with the thrust being made by the major beneficiaries of such a plan—create a seemingly unstoppable movement toward the cashless society.

Banking on the Future

Those who will benefit most from the cashless society are the institutions most pushing for it—the banking industry and card companies. The reasons all relate to increased profits. No matter how altruistic the rhetoric may sound, the bottom line is the bottom line.

For one thing, electronic banking is much cheaper for the bank. The costs are lower for processing electronic fund transfers than for processing checks and their related paper handling. In addition, money is moved much more quickly.

The following report shows a second major benefit to the card companies and banks.

Fifteen million Canadian VISA card holders charge more to their plastic money than the per capita average in all countries but Iceland.

"We're up to $35 billion in purchases per year, about $2,300 per card for everything from shirts to shishkabobs and root canals to telephone calls from airplanes.

"We've become an integral part of our customers' everyday lives," says Roger Woodward, president of VISA Canada. "VISA still hasn't edged out cash. But when it's cash we spend, untold billions comes from automated teller machines activated by VISA cards, here or at airports and hotels across the globe.

"In the minds of marketers at VISA and its member banks, there is still plenty of scope to displace cash and cheques, to become the world's top currency." Internationally, the VISA network aims to double transaction values to $1 trillion (U.S.) per year by the year 2000.[12]

In other words, by eliminating cash the bank-card companies will get a piece of all transactions conducted anywhere in the world. As creators of the system, their three to seven percent royalty will be their just reward.

Banks Take Interest

Many people may wonder why the banks would like a prepaid or immediate-paid (debit) system, since they make so much of their money from the interest charges on unpaid balances. Rest assured, the banks have not overlooked this lucrative revenue stream.

With the new debit card systems, consumers can go into an "overdraft" situation if preapproved by their bank. The difference is that the interest will begin to accrue immediately rather than at the end of the 25-to-30-day grace periods most credit cards allow. That means this source of revenue is still open to the banking industry and will result in increased profitability for the banks and credit card companies.

But far and away the greatest benefit to the banks is the elimination of the bank branch. William R. Woods of the Bank of Montreal said that most banks are expanding the number of ATM locations to provide easier access for their customers. With the increase of ATMs and their 24-hour accessibility, the necessity for bank branches is all but eliminated.

It is extremely costly for banks to staff multiple facilities and to pay for building upkeep. ATMs, which can perform almost all the functions of a branch bank, are vastly less expensive. A *USA Today* reporter, writing about the cost efficiency of ATMs in a story about their increased numbers and capabilities, wryly noted that ATMs don't ask for raises and don't need medical insurance.[13]

When a bank opens a branch, it has to hire architects, builders, contractors, electricians, pay building fees, and buy other permits. It has to furnish the bank, hire staff, train these employees, continually hire and retrain personnel, and pay continuous overhead. With an ATM, it has only to scout out a location like a mall, grocery store, or subway stop and send someone out once a day to service it—obviously, a lot cheaper.

The increased profitability and reduced branch bank costs are major incentives to the banking industry to push the cashless society to the forefront of tomorrow's world.

The Prime Movers

While consumers are beginning to be lured by the cashless convenience and retailers are discovering the cost effectiveness of the debit card system, and while banks continue their never-ending search for greater profits, society itself is finding reasons to embrace this new paper-free world.

Much of this support has come from law enforcement agencies. One of the most persuasive arguments for a cashless society is the effect it will have in deterring crime. At the street level, mugging will become unprofitable as fewer and fewer citizens carry cash. As more and more retailers deal in card sales only, profitable targets for armed robbers will cease to exist.

On a much larger scale, law enforcement experts boldly proclaim that drug trafficking can be all but eliminated in a cashless society. Drug dealers carry out their business one suitcase full of cash at a time. No credit cards, no cashier's checks—just cash. As cash is eliminated from everyday use, the medium of exchange for dealers vanishes. Large-scale transactions cannot be done through electronic banking without attracting the attention of bank officials and, in turn, law enforcement and other arms of government.

> *We are told that with the disappearance of cash will come also the disappearance of much crime. No wonder mankind will press for such a utopian economic system!*

Black-market activities also will be severely curtailed in a cashless society. Extortion, kidnapping, blackmail, and prostitution will be all but eradicated as currency is retired. We are told that with the disappearance of cash will come also the disappearance of much crime. No wonder mankind will press for such a utopian economic system!

No Paper Trail

A letter to the editor in *Time* magazine represents the prevailing attitude:

> Your report on drug smugglers converting drug-tinged money into clean assets shows that our government's over supply of U.S. currency is a prime cause of the growth of the cocaine trade. You explain that 80 percent of all the bills printed by the Treasury can't be located because so many of them are concealed by the dealers. As an assistant prosecutor at the county

level, I am disheartened by the inaction on denying the drug kings their medium of exchange, currency. One way to catch them would be a surprise big-cash recall. Let's demonetize the drug trade.[14]

Another particularly clear description of the problem and the solution was given by a career foreign-services officer:

> William G. Ridgeway isn't so immodest as to suppose his plan would save the world. All he claims for it is that it would bust up organized crime, put an end to the deadly traffic in illegal drugs, reduce espionage and terrorism, drastically curtail corruption and tax evasion and begin a return to civility.
>
> Ridgeway's plan (dubbed Bold $troke) would eliminate cash in favor of computerized, theft-proof "smart cards."
>
> Cash . . . is the criminal's vital accomplice, "the very mother's milk of the spy, the terrorist, the thief, the drug pusher, the drug user, the tax evader and the embezzler." Because it leaves no paper trail, it is "the interface between the legal and illegal world."[15]

Capitalizing on Fear

As crime in our society continues to increase, so does the draw to the plastic world. The number of stores accepting plastic money is increasing. Visa has signed up more than 3,000 supermarkets to take its cards. That's about half of the top 50 grocery chains in the United States.[16]

Even post offices in most U.S. cities are accepting credit cards as payment for postage. According to a news brief before the implementation of the system:

> After a two-year test, the United States Postal Service will start taking credit cards and debit cards in its offices nationwide. It promises to put card processing machines in many of its offices nationwide . . . The national rollout will constitute one of the largest single commitments to plastic ever.[17]

Other governmental agencies are getting into the act by using electronic payment systems for Social Security and welfare to help cut costs. One area of cost savings is found in the area of welfare fraud. Attempts are also being made to curb food stamp fraud by replacing the coupon system with plastic cards.

When paying for groceries, food stamp customers would run their cards through an electronic reader and would enter their personal identification number (PIN). Their account or card would then be debited for the purchase. Each month the food stamp recipient gets additional money stored on the card. This plan results in significant savings by stopping fraud. Recipients can't sell coupons to raise cash for the purchase of alcohol, drugs, or tobacco. The card can be used only by the person to whom it is issued. The cardholder is identified through some kind of link to the card such as a PIN.

Another benefit for the welfare recipient is the elimination of negative stereotyping attached to the use of food stamps. Use of many types of cards would mean that other customers would not know if someone was using a food stamp card, a credit card, or some other form of electronic payment. Thus the stigma of being "a welfare mother" or "deadbeat" that often accompanies food stamp use is eliminated and the user's privacy is protected.

Governments have become one of the biggest advocates for the elimination of cash and checks, especially in the Western world. Millions of dollars could be saved each month if government payments to individuals could be handled electronically rather than by issuing and processing expensive paper checks. Too, electronic deposits would put an end to the theft of Social Security and other government checks from the mail.

Tax evasion also would become a thing of the past. Cash payments for work performed or for items sold and other cash loopholes would be eliminated. This is a major priority among Western governments, particularly in the United States, which is facing staggering deficits. The estimated increase in tax revenue resulting from closing the floodgates of tax evasion would make a major dent in the deficit. In fact, a recent report estimates that if tax evaders alone could be thwarted, it would put at least an additional 100 billion dollars a year into U.S. government coffers.[18]

As national boundaries are beginning to fade in what is obviously becoming a global society, international governments would benefit from the elimination of foreign currency exchanges. Travelers would no longer have to stop every other hour in Europe to exchange currencies.

The list seems to go on and on. Retailers and consumers are becoming more comfortable with electronic banking—even in some cases preferring debit cards to the dinosaur of cash. Governments and banks are conducting impressive and effective public relations campaigns for this all-but-certain transition to cashlessness. Can the switch from cash to cards be far off?

It seems that almost every segment of modern society is creating a demand for these changes. Their reasons are sound, financially speaking. On the surface, the cashless society appears to be a win-win situation. Everyone will benefit from going cashless.

Or so it would seem . . .

3

||||||

What's in the
Cards?

A reporter friend once interviewed a small-time burglar about his knack for entering houses. The thief confided that most door locks could be compromised easily by inserting a small plastic card between the door jamb and the bolt. Presto! The door was open. "With a credit card, I can get anything I want," the burglar said with a devilish smile.

Although he surely didn't intend his statement to be used in the way we're going to use it, there is a remarkable similarity between his words and what we are going to be showing you in this chapter. Today, it can truly be said that you can get almost anything with a plastic card. And it's legal.

The technological advances of the past ten years in the card industry are almost incomprehensible. Credit cards, debit cards, and the like can, when used in an ATM or similar machine, provide us (like they did the thief) with immediate access to almost any service, product, or bit of information we might want. And the "new, improved, and smarter" cards can do even more.

A Full Deck of Cards

To begin, let's briefly consider the type of cards now on the market—not types as in credit or debit cards, but types as in the technical construction of the cards. As we will see, this is an important distinction.

Today, it can truly be said that you can get almost anything with a plastic card. And it's legal.

Magnetic Stripe Cards. These are the most commonly used cards in North America. They are a simple plastic credit or debit card with a black stripe on the back which contains certain information: perhaps your name, an account number, and a personal identification number called a PIN. When you go to an automated teller machine, you insert your card into the machine and punch in your PIN on the keypad. Once the machine verifies that the PIN you have punched matches the PIN recorded on the magnetic stripe card, you are then able to conduct a financial transaction such as withdrawing from or depositing funds to your account.

Smart Cards. These too are plastic credit or debit cards that contain a small microchip, usually in the top left corner. There are two types of smart cards. One is a memory-only card from which information can be obtained by a reading device. The information cannot be changed or updated. The other type has a microprocessor which allows for information to be updated, changed, or processed. According to Stephen Seidman, editor of *Smart Card Monthly*, the only real difference between this type of smart card and a personal computer is the packaging. Smart cards, like the magnetic stripe cards, must have some type of identification device (like a PIN) to match the cardholder with the card.

Optical Cards. These plastic cards contain data stored on the entire surface of the card, which can be read by laser. They store great amounts of data and are frequently used to store medical information. However, they seem the second-best choice when compared to the technology of the smart card.

While each of these cards could be capable of being *the* card in a cashless society, they all share one common drawback. To this date, no system has been developed to make certain that the person using the card is the person who should be using the card. The system of PINs simply has not worked, and the banks underwriting the system are losing a small fortune because of it.

Banks Are Big Losers

Automated teller machines and the entire plastic card industry are being ripped off at a staggering rate. Thieves use their victims' ATM cards to withdraw large amounts of cash (usually up to the daily limit) from the accounts. Cards are being counterfeited. And in both cases banks, not customers, are responsible for these losses and are losing millions of dollars each year.

Let's first look at the problem of card counterfeiting and how it is spurring the industry into trading in the traditional magnetic stripe cards for the new "smart" cards.

Card Counterfeiting: It's Where the Money's At

Magnetic stripe cards, the current industry standard, are easily counterfeited and the losses are stacking up. In fact, counterfeiting credit cards is considered the fastest-growing type of credit card crime in Canada, according to the Canadian Bankers' Association. One industry source said recently that counterfeiting accounts for about 14 percent of all credit card crime.[1]

Bankers say they aren't charging their legitimate customers for the counterfeit claims but are absorbing the losses themselves. This is highly unlikely. Either way, this counterfeiting has greatly increased an already massive security problem for North American banks. Credit card crime increased more than 50 percent in Canada from 1990 to 1991.

Visa and MasterCard lost about $50 million in 1991 on the 25 million cards in circulation in Canada.[2] Canadian crime statistics showed that about 50,000 credit cards ended up in the hands of thieves in 1991 alone.[3]

Smart Cards to the Rescue

Sid Price, senior vice-president of the National Processing Company, the largest credit card processing company in the United States, says the next logical step is to convert the U.S. card structure to a smart card system.

It has long been argued that the cost of making this major change would be too great. But with the losses increasing each year, many people are saying the United States cannot afford *not* to make the change. The demand for change has reached a level that prompts Price to predict that the crossover is "only months away, not years."[4]

The primary impetus for this change is, of course, to eliminate the losses incurred by credit card fraud. The consensus among industry leaders is that smart cards are virtually impossible to counterfeit or duplicate. And they have built-in mechanisms that make them "hacker proof."

Smart cards look just like the plastic credit cards that have been around for years, but they contain a small computer chip which appears as a gold dot on the card instead of the black stripe. Although these cards have not "caught on" in North America like they have in Europe, the United States is on the threshold of not only taking a giant step into this technology, but of also actually becoming the industry leader.

MAC Makes a Major Move

This possibility comes on the heels of an announcement in October 1992 by MAC (Money Access System), the operator of the largest electronic funds transfer network in the United States. MAC announced that starting in 1994, all of its 932 member financial institutions would have access to the first mass market smart card system in the United States. Member institutions at the time of the announcement had about 26 million cardholders.[5]

The overriding business plan behind this system is a desire for a slice of the 30 billion transactions currently carried out in the United States each year at a value of under ten dollars. These transactions are now predominantly cash and MAC cannot derive any revenue from them.

By launching the cash card system, the company can now look forward to opening up a huge, untapped market for its switching business.[6]

Visa Making a Big Change, Too

Visa has announced that it is prepared to move into the smart card market. Despite long-standing opposition to the smart card, Visa officials have now acknowledged that "smart cards are a reliable and proven technology." Visa is still considering using smart cards with PINs, but the biometric industry is hoping to change Visa's mind about card security.[7]

We'll talk more about biometrics and card security a little later.

Visa will undoubtedly play a major role in bringing the smart card to America. It already has 34 million debit cards in circulation and plans to have 100 million in circulation by 1994.[8]

Meanwhile, it is projected the European Community will have another 200 million smart cards in the market by 1994. That figure will drastically increase to about 500 million in the next three years, experts at TRT-Phillips predicted. The same report shows that worldwide the figures will be 308 million "memory only" smart cards by 1994—30 million of which will contain microprocessors. By 1996, those figures are projected to be 675 million with 40 million containing microprocessors.[9]

More Than Just Money

So far we have talked primarily about the smart cards and how they will ultimately replace cash. But there are many other applications for the card. Stephen Seidman, publisher of *Smart Card Monthly*, gives us additional perspectives on the capabilities of the smart cards.

> From a business point of view, IC/ Smart Cards are now being used to identify employees and guests, automate time and attendance records, control access to parking lots, buildings . . . copiers, fax machines, corporate records. . . . As money, they are used to collect and balance travel

expenses via company-installed ATMs, to make purchases in company stores and in neighboring shops, and shopping malls.[10]

Seidman continues:

Nationally—in degrees varying from country to country—cards are being used, and/or planned for imminent use, in national public telephone systems, health care, and financial transaction processing networks.[11]

An American National ID Card?

Recently, the Clinton administration announced interest in the implementation of a health card as part of the reform of the health care system in the United States. In the September 1992 edition of the *New England Journal of Medicine*, then-governor Bill Clinton was quoted as saying, "Everyone will carry smart cards coded with his or her personal medical information."[12]

The implementation of a smart health card would obviously alter the entire smart card market in the United States. And when we consider how many personal documents the smart card can eliminate or store in one place, it sounds even more appealing. To date, no governmental agency or business has fully endorsed such an all-encompassing card, but it seems so practical that it's probably inevitable.

It's the Big MAC

Remember a little earlier when we talked about the changes in the MAC system's cards? The company said it had no firm plans to expand its smart card to a full, multifunctional one. Yet, MAC chose one of the top-of-the-line smart cards available, the Gemplus 16 Kb EEPROM MCOS. This card, according to *Card Technology Today*, is equipped with a microprocessor and an operating system specifically aimed at handling multiple applications.[13]

We've already mentioned the large amount of information these little cards can hold and how many separate identification cards could be eliminated by one smart card. It is difficult to imagine just how much information one of these microprocessors can hold—yet the microprocessor in a smart card is about one-sixth the size of a postage stamp!

What a Powerful Little Item

Just how powerful are these microprocessors? We asked our research staff to look into that question. The conclusions?

The U.S. government is exploring the use of smart card technology for its proposed universal health card, because the microchip in a smart card can retain incredible amounts of information. A 4 meg chip, quite common today, can hold the equivalent of 16,000 pages of single space text! That would be more than ample to carry a person's entire health history [even a very old and very sickly person], not to mention insurance information, all on a chip 1/6th the size of a postage stamp.[14]

As amazing as this is, hold onto your hat. Here's the rest of the story.

But the big news is the latest chip that was announced for the first time at the Global Frontier conference. Toshiba has developed a microprocessor chip, no larger than the 4 meg chip, that can retain up to one gigabyte of information for up to 100 years!

What in the world is a gigabyte? Basically, a "byte" is the smallest measurement of computer data, roughly equal to 1/6th of an alphabetic character, such as a "T." For example, to type the word "type" takes roughly 24 bytes. Earlier we spoke of a 4 meg chip holding 16,000 pages of information. 4 meg is four million "bytes." A gigabyte is a billion bytes.

To give you some sense of perspective, one million seconds is 12 days. One billion seconds is 32 years. A gigabyte of memory is equal to 10,000 times an average personal computer's capacity.[15]

Isn't that incredible? Today these uncounterfeitable cards hold the potential to serve as the world's first fully functional "electronic wallet." The largest single stumbling block to the system is still the problem of making sure that the person using the card is the person to whom it belongs.

The real source of these problems, as we've said, is the present security system used by the banks. The system relies on personal identification numbers as its only security procedure.

Today these uncounterfeitable cards hold the potential to serve as the world's first fully functional "electronic wallet."

A PIN is assigned to the cardholder when he or she receives the card. This four-digit number is encoded in the card and given to the cardholder. When making an ATM transaction, the cardholder inserts the card into the ATM and then types in his secret number. If that number matches the one stored on the card, the machine assumes that the person using the card is the rightful owner. It sounds pretty good in theory, but in practice it simply isn't working.

PINs Aren't Real Secure

The PIN is usually randomly selected by the card manufacturer, although in some cases the customers select their own number. Often cardholders select a PIN that is easy for them to remember—like a birthday (5-3-45), the last four digits of their Social Security number (4832), the last four digits of their phone number (8037), or some other familiar number. The problem with this is that these numbers are probably located on other documents in the victim's purse or wallet. Thieves will look for these familiar numbers and try them on the keypad, often with success. *U.S. News & World Report* sums up the problem:

> In an era when virtually all Americans are asked to show I.D. ranging from driver's licenses to credit cards, the process of insuring that a person is who he or she claims to be is big business and a matter of growing concern. No longer is the simple password, the I.D. badge or the magnetic encoded card sufficient, say security experts. Those traditional devices can be falsified, stolen or discovered accidentally.[16]

Banks strongly caution customers to memorize their PIN and then destroy the card that contains their security number. But that doesn't happen often enough.

Many elderly card users don't trust their memories, so they write the PIN down and carry it with them. Unfortunately, they often carry the number in their wallet or purse near the card itself and clearly identify the number as their ATM PIN. Many card users—and not just the elderly or the mentally impaired—actually write their PIN on the card!

They make it so easy for the thief. A study by the Federal Reserve Bank of Atlanta documented this sad reality:

> Current norms of security . . . in general have failed to provide much more than a rudimentary link between the individual and his access to funds in his account. . . . The magnetic strip card combination merely seeks to match a holder of the plastic card with the knowledge of a four to six digit code or PIN.
>
> A growing body of research indicated, ironically, that many card holders—rather than memorize a PIN—carry a written copy of their PIN near their bank card. Others literally write their PIN directly on their plastic card.[17]

Another problem with the current PIN security system involves armed robberies. Any reasonable person held at gunpoint will gladly cough up a PIN rather than be shot.

Currently the losses from these security shortfalls have been minimized by daily limits set on the amount of money a person can withdraw from the ATMs. At our banks the limits are $500 per day. Thus, if someone stole one of our bankcards and somehow managed to find the corresponding PIN number, he could only do minimal damage before the theft was reported.

It is clear that if we are to move to a cashless society, a better, more secure card system has to be developed. There is simply no other choice.

The report of the Federal Reserve Bank of Atlanta referred to a moment ago noted that "some alternatives [are] being considered, such as signature dynamics and voice recognition [which] are based on non-transferable, biometric characteristics."[18] These characteristics, which also include fingerprints, are a means of certifying that you really are who you say you are. In this electronic world, even our fingerprints can be integrated into a computer database. As we'll see, this is all leading closer and closer to the world of the mark of the beast.

4

Your Body:
The Only ID
You'll Ever Need

His name is Bond. James Bond. And to gain access to his secret headquarters he might place his finger in an electronic machine that verifies that he is indeed 007. Or to get into a NATO compound he might look into a pair of goggles that resemble binoculars. As he does so, a light beam focuses on the vein patterns in his eyes, patterns which are even more unique than his fingerprints.

While James Bond is pure fiction, these space-age technologies are now very much a part of the real world. Known collectively as biometrics, these systems identify a person by unique physical or behavioral characteristics. When perfected, undoubtedly these systems will hold the key to the ultimate security of the electronic world.

Today, leading-edge biometric technologies include fingerprint readers, hand geometry machines, retinal readers, voice recognition systems, signature dynamics, and a myriad of others. In a world where cash is eliminated and every financial transaction is done electronically, security is the critical factor in both running the system and in getting people to put their trust in it. Biometrics may still sound futuristic, but in today's fast-moving world the future is now.

Bud Goes Shopping

For the sake of clarity allow us to introduce a fictional character, Bud. Let's pretend he is participating in a fingerprint verification program with his new debit smart card. Bud has decided to take this path because he can never quite remember his personal identification number. To get things rolling, Bud heads down to the local grocery store where the card company has an "enrollment counter" set up.

In a world where cash is eliminated and every financial transaction is done electronically, security is the critical factor in both running the system and in getting people to put their trust in it.

At the counter Bud is issued his own smart card with its tiny microchip. The card is programmed as a debit card so that when Bud later arrives at the checkout counter with his groceries, the money can be electronically transferred from Bud's bank account to the store's. But now, back at the enrollment counter, something else has to take place before Bud can begin his shopping.

Bud is asked by the young lady doing the enrollment to put his finger in a tiny machine hooked up to a personal computer. This machine scans his fingerprint and makes a computer picture of it called a template. In just a few seconds that template is digitally transferred and stored in the memory of the computer chip in Bud's smart card. That's it. The job is done. It all took under five minutes.

May I Have Your Card and Your Finger, Please?

Now Bud is ready to do his shopping. Five jars of peanut butter, two bunches of bananas, and a side of beef fill his cart and he's off to the checkout counter. When it's time to pay, Bud hands his smart card to the salesclerk who places it in the point of sale (POS) terminal which is electronically linked to Bud's bank and the store's bank. Instantly, the money is transferred from Bud's bank account and placed in the store's. But, wait—what if it is not Bud who is presenting this card? After all, the clerk doesn't know him. He might be using someone else's card.

To verify that Bud is indeed the owner of the card, the clerk asks him to put his finger in the reader attached to the POS terminal. This reader scans Bud's fingerprint, just as the reader at the enrollment counter did. But now, it compares that fingerprint to the one stored on the card. If the two match, Bud can make his purchase. If not, the police will quickly be on their way.

The combination of smart cards and biometric security is a technological marriage with great potential.

What an ingenious system! No number to memorize. No hassle—all you need is your card and your finger. It's just that simple and secure.

This Is Not Onboard the Enterprise

These technological advances may sound like something out of a James Bond movie or an episode of "Star Trek," but the fact is that the basics of biometric systems have been around for more than 20 years. Slow public acceptance and dwindling research funds impeded their development in the last decade, but the push is on again to make such systems a cost-effective reality. High development costs made the practicality of these systems suspect in the eighties, but survivors in this highly competitive field have been able to lower equipment costs and are convinced that the promises of the last decade will be a reality in this one.

Today, costs for card-based biometric POS systems have shrunk to between $3,500 and $7,000 each. And while they are more expensive than PIN systems, the realities of an electronic world are indeed making them more competitive:

> "Now that we are cost competitive, we feel that comparisons will be performance, not price, driven," said one industry official. "The person with all their billing records at stake doesn't really care if it costs $6,000 or $4,000. It's not really relevant."[1]

While these systems are expensive, in a world where cash is eliminated and every person's security is directly related to the security of the electronic system, it is a small price to pay.

Securing the New World Order

Because of their expense and their limited usefulness in the current cash- and credit-driven society, biometric security systems have been developed primarily for governments and clients who depend on high-security environments. But that is changing. A 1992 report estimated that biometric industry sales will double by 1995 to about $40 million.[2]

The largest of these new markets is in the area of smart card security. Stephen Seidman, publisher of *Smart Card Monthly*, says:

> I think certain applications are going to drive the growth of smart cards and biometrics together. Coupling the two allows for the identification of the card holder and, hence, unattended remote operations.[3]

The combination of smart cards and biometric security is a technological marriage with great potential. It's a union that is both logical and fiscally sound. After the initial outlay for biometric terminals, the system will no doubt result in substantial savings—at least for the banking and credit card industries. Surely, consumers and retailers will also share in these dividends.

According to Ben Miller, editor of *PIN: Personal Identification News*,

> Biometrics and smart cards have been implemented together in numerous programs during the past five years. . . . The concept of performing the biometric comparison in the smart card chip component is considered to be one of the most secure forms of protection for data and executable smart card functions. . . . In essence, the process is the same as PIN comparisons currently processed in most smart cards, but the security level is higher because hands, unlike PINs, cannot be lost, stolen or forgotten.[4]

You Are As Unique As the Computer Says You Are

Let's now take a closer look at the various biometric identifiers.

The most familiar biometric identifier is the fingerprint. Fingerprint identification has been a standard, especially in the legal system, for many years. This unique method of identification has progressed considerably in the past few years, thanks to technological advancements.

A leader in the industry claims that its latest system is the ultimate solution for identifying individuals:

> TouchSafe proves that a person is who he claims to be. This proof is simple and takes only a second. Each compact terminal contains a fingerprint reader connected to a processor board.[5]

Fingerprinting Still Jessica Fletcher's Choice

Law enforcement agencies have used fingerprint identification for a very long time. Old movies show the tired detective, a cigarette hanging from the corner of his mouth, flipping through fingerprint books trying to find a match. TV's Jessica Fletcher and her police cohorts, however, have no such problems. The old methods have been updated and simplified using new technology. Identification can therefore be much quicker, with instant access to computerized fingerprint files. No longer do people have to flip through stacks of fingerprint pictures; now the computer can do the comparisons for them at lightning speed. And it's still an almost foolproof method of identification.

But such systems are valuable not only for detectives and grocery shoppers; the uses are as diverse as one could imagine. Maryland's state police, for example, are using Identix fingerprint machines to ensure that the wrong prisoner is not released, which could be quite a problem under the old system. They are also interlinking their machines so that prisoners can be properly identified at certain checkpoints, like a courtroom, the infirmary, the pharmacy, and so forth. At many high-security prisons, even the visitors have to submit to electronic fingerprint verification.

> "We have people here that have a history of violence and escape," Leavenworth spokesman Dan McCauley said. "At any one time you have to figure that somebody is trying to plan some way to get out of this place, so your visiting becomes a security issue."

> Visitors to the prison will insert a finger into a small scanner. A record of the fingerprint will then be stored on a computerized database along with the prints of other prison visitors.

"When you come out you'll put your finger in the system again and it will say 'Yep, that was you who went in and now you've checked out,'" said Scoot G. Schiller, director of investor relations for Fingermatrix. "What they're trying to protect here is that the wrong person doesn't leave."[6]

The SINS (Statewide Integrated Narcotics System) project sponsored by the California Department of Justice has also adopted fingerprint identification to secure individual computer work stations. This ensures that only authorized employees are allowed access to the data in ongoing investigations.

Alive or Dead? The Machine Can Tell

Someone might argue that this is OK for a prisoner who is under surveillance by an armed guard, but what about fingerprint identification for banking cards? What's to stop a criminal from killing his victim, cutting off the victim's finger, and then using it to access his financial accounts?

The new technology has an answer. When fingerprint devices are verifying a person's fingerprint, they can also tell if the finger is alive or dead. That might sound a little weird, but bear with us for a moment.

Most people would willingly place their finger in a fingerprint reader at the behest of an armed robber, but suppose a victim resisted and was murdered or otherwise incapacitated. In bizarre cases (where illegal entry is being attempted at high-security installations, for example) where the stakes are high, it is not implausible that a criminal might cut off a person's finger and use it in the security device.

It wouldn't work. At the 1993 Card Technology conference, a demonstrator of one of these finger-print security systems explained that the system can tell if a finger is dead by a hemoglobin reading built into the system.

Darling, Your Hands Are So Geometrical

While fingerprinting is still the most popular biometric method, many new developments are threatening its dominance. One of these is hand geometry.

Hand geometry has existed since 1971. In re-cent years it has become more popular as an iden-tification tool. Westinghouse Hanford's Company Security Application Center (SAC) has recently developed a template using hand geometry instead of the fingerprint. Just as in the case of the finger-print, the template is stored in the smart card and can be accessed for comparison at any time.

You've no doubt seen such devices in science fiction or spy thriller movies. To gain entry to a secured area, the employee seeking access must insert his hand in a reading device. Just like in the movies, today's hand scan machines verify the shape of the hand and the length and height of the fingers—minus, of course, the whirring sound and the pul-sating lights necessary for the movies.

Customs and Immigration to the Left, Hand Scans to the Right, Please

Hand geometry verification is a reality and is already in operation in many high-security facilities. In fact, just such a system has been installed in airports around the world. In two airports in the eastern United States, the system has been installed to speed up the immigration process. Here is how one newspaper described the new machines:

> Infrared hand scans... [which] take two to four seconds are said to be harmless (no x-rays are used) and 99 percent accurate in determining whether a passport belongs to the person presenting it.
>
> Here's how it works: A traveler walks up to an electronic inspection booth, inserts his passport into a document-reading machine, then puts his hand on a scanner that measures its geometry and reads such characteristics as the relationship of one finger to another.
>
> If the computer decides the passport and the passport holder match, the admission gate automatically opens.[7]

The article further says that the Immigration and Naturalization Service is planning to install such systems, depending on the results of these field tests, in all international airports in the United

States. These hand scanners are expected to reduce the traveler's reentry process to about 30 seconds—a considerable time savings when you consider that delays for passport checks can now take up to 90 minutes at the busiest airports. As the world becomes more globally interdependent, quick access across borders will be essential.

While these developments are interesting in themselves, there is another development which makes the system even more fascinating. New breakthroughs in the field of electronic passports may mean that the need for storing biometrics onto a plastic card is no longer necessary.

> The current feeling is that hand geometry templates could be stored in an OCR (Optical Character Recognition) format on newly issued visas or as a sticky label which could simply be stuck to the passport. Apart from the hand geometry verification units located at entry points, no new hardware would be required apart from OCR equipment, which has, in fact, already been installed at a number of airports around the world. [The traveler] will be asked to give a hand geometry sample . . . the resulting nine digit template will then be printed onto a sheet of paper which can be inserted into the passport. . . .
>
> The next time the passenger arrives at a participating airport, he will be able to go directly to the special self-service passport

control exit. The two part turnstile barrier located there will firstly require him to present the biometric template sheet so that the template details can be captured. He will then move on to the second part of the turnstile where he will be required to give a hand geometry reading. Provided the new sample compares adequately well with the template, he will be allowed to pass through into the main concourse.

Hand geometry can, then, offer a significant cost advantage. It is not only this capability to eliminate the need to issue a card or other device . . . but hand geometry verification has a second advantage in that it has the best all around performance in the biometric field.[8]

Hey Lady, How About a Little Less Hand Cream?

Hand geometry creates a template based on certain measurements and relationships unique to each person's hand. A geometric analysis might show the length of all the fingers as well as the normal space between the fingers at varying points while the hand is relaxed. The reading might also give the width of fingers, the width of the hand span, the width of the hand at the "heel" and a variety of other notations. These geometric readings are just as individualized as fingerprints.

Hand geometry also works where fingerprinting might not. For example, fingerprinting is very unreliable for certain people, such as manual workers, pipe smokers, and women who wear hand cream. In all of these instances, impressions left by the swirls and circles in normal fingerprints can be impossible to record because they are filled with a foreign substance (hand cream), have been burnt smooth (by constantly holding a hot pipe), or have been worn away by constant friction (caused by manual labor). Moreover, many biometric experts believe fingerprint technology may meet some resistance due to its long-standing association with criminal activities.

The one technical drawback to hand geometry is that it requires an individual to place his or her hand in a very precise location on the reading area. But this seems to be a temporary setback.

The Mark VI Personal Identity Verifier

Biometric Technology Today newsletter tells us that one company, PIDEAC, has recently gone into large-scale production of its Mark VI Personal Identity Verifier. The article says,

> This hand geometry verification device is unusual in that it does not require users to place their hands within posts or grooves located on the reading area. Instead, the company has developed a technique which allows the hand to be placed anywhere within the reading area. Both

hands can be enrolled in the system in case of injury to one in the future.[9]

The student of Bible prophecy will not only be interested in the name of this device, but in the fact that its developers have decided to record both hands in case of injury. The Bible may well have been foretelling just such a precaution when it referred to "marking" the right hand or forehead.

There are some other interesting features of the new Mark VI system as well. Not only can the device be used for ID verification, but it can be programmed with access time restrictions, with the names and employee numbers of authorized users, and with time and attendance records for payroll purposes.

This Mark VI system will be priced at about $6,300—not an exorbitant price when you consider the time-saving security measures it provides. But PIDEAC is currently testing a simpler and smaller device for low- or medium-security use which measures the length of only four fingers. These devices would cost less than $1,000. Besides their obvious uses, these smaller devices could be mounted on the dashboards of cars as antitheft devices or provide access and security in restricted parking areas.

I've Grown Accustomed to Your Face

Facial recognition is a fairly new biometric industry. At the "Solutions for the Global Frontier" conference in Washington, D.C., conference organizer Ben Miller pointed out that several companies are working on facial recognition devices. According to Miller, however, only one company, Neuro-Metric Vision, is close to developing a product that could be on the market soon.

> Facial recognition systems have been built that can recognize human faces that match those from a previously enrolled population. Most are limited to relatively small populations and have limited tolerance to size, orientation and lighting changes. Pattern recognition research is benefiting from advances in neural technology and in computer technology.

> "As techniques and tools continue to improve, facial recognition is almost certain to become a significant biometric technology," according to James P. Holmes of Sandia National Laboratories.[10]

Pat, I'll Take a Nose, an Eye, and an Ear for $300

A prototype of another related technology known as Visage also was shown during the conference. This system, although not as high tech as facial recognition, is an intriguing approach to identity verification.

> [This system may] not be a true biometric at all—its developer, Hugh Davis, has come up with the term physiognomic

as the best way of describing it. This is defined as the art of judging character from facial characteristics. . . . This is not exactly what Visage actually does, [but] it is the closest term that could be found!

To enroll on the Visage system, users must pick three different facial images. These could be of two people known to the user and one stranger chosen by the computer or all three could be chosen by the computer. At the time of verification, eight similar but different faces to one of those chosen by the user, along with his chosen face, appear on a screen in random positions in a three by three matrix. Shown next to each face is a letter and the user must press the correct letter for his chosen face. If the correct face has been identified, then the screen brings up a further nine faces. The user again picks his chosen face and a further set of nine faces are again displayed for him to choose from.

Although Visage may seem a cumbersome approach, tests indicate that it is actually quite quick. The faces are shown for only 1-2 seconds—just long enough for the right person to select their three correct faces. It was also found that people could easily remember their faces after three months, long after they had forgotten a PIN. The only time that people were rejected by the system was when they miskeyed their choices. The system was designed with the needs of the computer access control market in mind, but it is believed that further development could make it suitable for other biometric application areas.[11]

Is It Live or Is It Memorex?

As is generally the case in developing industries, these technologies are not the only ones evolving. Recent Hollywood movies have introduced to the public all the latest designs. Voice verification systems, for example, are being fine-tuned.

Those who have seen the movie "Sneakers" will recall that it was through the use of recorded voice patterns that the heroes defeated the voice verification system. This technology is advancing, but as in the movie, there are still bugs in the system. Would a system be able to distinguish between a "live" voice or a recorded one? Could a voice recognition system know the answer to the question, "Is it live or is it Memorex?" Developers say that the real systems can "baffle even digital voice recording" but also admit that a second security verifier (like a PIN) is advisable.

As an indication of how far this technology has advanced, researchers at universities and in the private sector are developing personal computers that operate by voice recognition—not for the purposes of identification, but to translate spoken words into written words. Already, we have entered the Star Trek age where accessing your computer can be as simple as saying, "Computer."

Your Personal Bar Code

Other identity verification systems are being studied by a myriad of researchers. One of the most interesting is called vein checking. When your fist is clenched, the veins on the subcutaneous part of the hand are more visible to the naked eye and even more so to vein-detection devices. This technique already has been dubbed "the personal bar code."[12]

At the same time, the Pentagon is experimenting with a new genetic identification system. Military officials say that, once in place, the system will guarantee there will be no more "unknown soldier" casualties in future wars. According to an Associated Press story, the Department of Defense has:

> authorized the creation of a repository of biological samples, taken from the blood and oral swabs of all armed services members, that could be used for identification. Army Maj. Victor Weeden, (folo) chief of the Armed Forces Institute of pathology, said the samples will be placed on identification cards that will be stored in vacuum-sealed packages and then frozen.[13]

Built Just the Way You Like It

Despite these remarkable developments, implementation of this technology is hindered by two factors: public acceptance and the high cost of the equipment. The first problem is beginning to wane. *Biometric Technology Today* reports that Barclays Bank has been conducting biometric tests, and the reaction of the public has been surprisingly positive:

> Barclays' interest in testing fingerprint verification systems has been given a significant boost by the results of the consumer reaction to a biometrics project carried out in September, 1992.
>
> The research was carried out by the Plastic Card Fraud Prevention Forum (PFPF), under the auspices of the British banking association, APACS. BTT has seen excerpts from the APACS report on this research which gives some surprising results. Two thousand people from a cross-section of the population were asked their opinion on the use of PINs, signature verification and fingerprint verification at the point-of-sale.
>
> Fingerprint verification systems emerged as the surprise favorite method of verification overall out of the three approaches included in the survey. The main reason for this was its perceived high level of security. Fingerprint verification was also seen as fast, reliable and easy to use.[14]

Clearly, when the public perceives additional safety for themselves and their finances and the possibility of reduced bank card and retail charges, their fear of such Orwellian devices seems to decrease.

Say Hello to Tomorrow

These elaborate systems certainly seem logical and are certain to have some positive long-term effects. Costs are coming down. Just think back to the days when calculators first came on the market. Our friend Arno Froese, president of Midnight Call Ministries, tells a story about the time he purchased his first calculator. It took a salesman a whole morning to demonstrate this new technology, which at that time was quite expensive. Now, of course, you can purchase calculators at a discount store's checkout display for a couple of dollars. Likewise XTs (IBM's original personal computers) are now considered the world's youngest antique.

So while researchers continue to develop the hardware and software for these verification systems, others in science, industry, and government are fervently seeking a better, more cost-effective, and even more secure system—one that will have universal feasibility, accessibility, and capability. With the world's financial future hanging in the balance, it's no longer a question of "if," only of "when."

5

‖‖‖‖

Will That Be
Hand or Forehead?

Here's a simple trick: Wave your hand over the computer scanner at the grocery store checkout counter, and your bill is deducted from your checking account. The technology to accomplish [this] feat already is here . . . said Tim Willard, executive director of the World Future Society, a Washington organization that claims 27,000 members worldwide. But the will may not be.

"Just suggest something like an implant in humans and the social outcry is tremendous," Willard said. "While people over the years may have grown accustomed to artificial body parts, there is definitely a strong aversion to things being implanted. It's the big brother is watching concept: People would be afraid that all their thoughts and movements were being monitored."[1]

The above quotation did not come from a Christian magazine or a prophetic newsletter. Instead it was a news release of the respected Gannett News Service. Moreover, reports like this one are not isolated or farfetched.

In this electronic world, the security of the computerized system is of paramount concern. In that light, no precaution seems too extreme.

The greatest problem facing cashless planners is making sure the person with the smart card in his pocket is the person to whom it rightfully belongs.

To the student of Bible prophecy, however, this is where a discussion of the cashless society, smart cards, and biometrics comes full circle. Suddenly, the leading-edge ideas of twentieth-century security planners line up with prophecies recorded by the apostle John some 2,000 years ago.

And make no mistake about it—this technology is coming whether we like it or not. Listen to the words of Terry Galanoy, the former director of communications for (what is today) Visa International.

> Protesting too loudly about it isn't going to help either, because the disturbance you kick up is going to end up in one of your files. And on that come-and-get-it day when we're all totally and completely dependent upon our card—*or whatever security device might replace it*—you might be left all alone without one![2]

Now, compare that warning and the Gannett release quoted previously to a passage from the book of Revelation.

> And he causeth all, both small and great, rich and poor, free and bond, to receive a mark in their right hand, or in their foreheads: And that no man might buy or sell, save he that had the mark, or the name of the beast, or the number of his name (Revelation 13:16,17).

As always, God is way ahead of the latest biometric engineers, smart card developers, and global communication systems planners. It boggles the mind! God is not dead; much to the contrary, He is more on top of the latest world events than all of the misguided philosophers who prepared His obituary.

Will That Be Hand or Forehead?

Think about it for a moment. It's ingenious. The greatest problem facing cashless planners is making sure the person with the smart card in his pocket is the person to whom it rightfully belongs. But the smart card is not really a card at all. All that is smart about it is the tiny microchip glued to it. The rest of the plastic card is just a handy carrying case and a Madison-Avenue-like attempt to make us all comfortable by giving us this new technology packaged in the same plastic cards we've become used to.

But what if you simply took the microchip from the card and implanted it under the skin? Presto, you no longer need all these sophisticated biometric devices. You don't need to verify that the person with the card is the rightful owner. The person *is* the card!

We'll talk a little more about that in a few moments, but first let's open our minds to the realities of implementing such a system. The great problem, as we have seen, is in getting people to accept such an ominous-sounding system. As is so often the case, however, hundreds of reasons seem to be cropping up to convince planners and ordinary citizens that implants may be one of the finest ideas in human history.

Do You Know Where Your Kids Are?

In the 1980s, we became alarmingly aware that

thousands of our children were missing. Our sensibilities were assaulted with gruesome reports of youngsters being stolen for use in pagan rituals and in the child pornography industry as well as becoming targets of sexual molestation and misuse by those in what is called the "white slavery" business. Add to this kidnappings for ransoms and abductions by estranged parents, and the problem took on monumental proportions.

Milk cartons and heart-wrenching television advertisements were a constant reminder that every day children were being abducted, abused, and often murdered. This drastic problem led to equally desperate proposals to halt the increase in such criminal activity. Many methods of tracking abducted children or runaways were suggested.

One was Kiddie Alert, a transmitter that fastens to a child's clothing and triggers an alarm if the child wanders beyond a preset distance (up to 200 feet), or if the transmitter is immersed in water or removed.[3] Effective, but not foolproof. The sound of the alarm could be muffled or the device could be turned off as easily by the perpetrator as by the parent.

A similar security system has been developed for newborns:

> You've seen them used in stores to stop shoplifting. Now some hospitals are using electronic security devices to protect more precious commodities: newborns. Amid concern about infant abductions, more and more babies are wearing sensor bracelets until they go home.[4]

This is a clever plan and might alleviate the problem a little, but someone intent on snatching a newborn from the relatively secure environment of a hospital is probably aware of security measures and will merely disarm or remove the device.

Despite these ingenious ideas, one solution is viewed by most technocrats as the ultimate—the use of implants. It is the most secure of all the plans suggested to date. One of the first to propose such a scheme was a plastic surgeon in Florida:

> A tiny homing device implanted behind the ear will help parents locate their missing children, says a plastic surgeon who developed the gadget using the same technology that led to cellular phones. The device, which emits electronic signals, could also help law enforcement officials find parolees and aid in the search for victims of Alzheimer's disease who have wandered off, said the developer, Dr. Daniel Mann. Private industry and government agencies have expressed interest in the mini-beeper, which measures less than an inch in size. Mann was awarded a patent ... for the device, which would work on an electronic energy system. The gadget emits a signal that could be monitored through a cellular system or possibly by satellite. Reaction has been generally positive.[5]

While it could possibly serve as the solution to

one of our most pressing societal problems, developers acknowledge that "without a doubt, this device would be the ultimate invasion of privacy because they [the authorities] would be able to find you anytime they want."[6]

They argue, however, that this disadvantage must be weighed against the greater good—the welfare of our children. This is such a powerful argument that it's opening the door to increased and widespread use of this ominous technology.

Oh, to Be Young Again

It would be one thing if at-risk children were the only group being considered for such implants, but today many voices in a variety of fields are calling for implants in large portions of the population.

An implant strategy, for example, could keep better tabs on victims of Alzheimer's disease who often lose track of their surroundings and wander off. Our local radio station often airs news bulletins asking listeners to be on the lookout for "a man dressed in a white jacket, blue pajama bottoms and green slippers." It breaks our heart every time we hear it. Tragically, many die from exposure before they are found. It is estimated that there are more than 75,000 chronic wanderers in the United States alone.[7]

At the request of five federal agencies involved with the problems of the elderly, the Research Triangle Institute of North

Carolina is studying the efficacy of attaching small transmitters to chronic wanderers.[8]

"This Week in Bible Prophecy" camera crews recently visited one nursing home to see how its staff dealt with this problem. As in so many other nursing homes, we found that the residents were fitted with a wrist or ankle bracelet that activates an alarm if they wander off. It's doubtful anyone would propose implants for just this purpose, but if such implants were used for other reasons, this could certainly be an added use.

Prison Security Improved

Severely overcrowded prisons plague our society. One innovative solution to this problem is a program that keeps nonviolent prisoners in a prison within their own home. These electronic leash programs are run under the same principle as the system used to keep children safe at home.

The prisoner is fitted with a nonremovable electronic bracelet while a base unit is placed in the house. If the prisoner (and the electronic bracelet) wanders beyond set limits, the base unit calls the police. Under such programs, described as "electronic prison bars" or "electronic leashes," many nonviolent prisoners are now serving their sentences at home! The prisoners' movements are monitored electronically by impulses given off by a transmitter in the bracelet that alerts police if the criminal wanders beyond the preset limits.

At the time of this writing, Dr. Jack Kevorkian, the so-called suicide doctor, has been released from custody but has had an electronic bracelet attached to his leg to make sure that he does not leave his home and help with any more suicides.

The primary purpose of electronic leashes was never to reduce crime, as is often mistakenly implied. These monitoring devices are being tested in various locations as a way to reduce overcrowded conditions in prisons. There remain some drawbacks to the system, however. Once the prisoner leaves the monitored area, what he does—legally or illegally—can't be tracked. Here's a good example from a Michigan newspaper:

> A man who authorities say committed an estimated 90 break-ins while serving time on an electronic tether pleaded guilty to three breaking and entering charges.
>
> The break-ins occurred on weekends when [the prisoner], hooked to an electronic tether for a previous sentence, had five hours each day for personal use, authorities said.[9]

The system is certainly not foolproof. But it is easing overcrowded conditions in prisons, and the practice is increasing every year, according to J.B. Vaughn, a criminal justice professor at Central Missouri State University. Professor Vaughn, preparing a report for the U.S. Justice Department, noted that electronic monitoring programs are growing rapidly. The number of prisoners being monitored by such devices increased from only 95 in 1986 to approximately 65,650 in 1993.[10]

Uses for these devices are being hailed as near-perfect solutions to nearly impossible situations. Unfortunately, some grave concerns are being ignored (more on that later). Extending such a system to read implanted microprocessors would also be a great asset for police officers on patrol. Vital information about the suspect they have arrested would immediately be available so necessary precautions could be taken.

OK, Mister, Drop the Gun

Louder calls for gun control are coming on the heels of increased crime. According to a report in *USA Today*, "A personal smart card that every citizen would carry is just one controversial idea the Justice Department has to keep guns out of felons' hands."[11] The Justice Department also has suggested that gun shops install high-tech fingerprint scanners.

Personal freedom and individual privacy are at the heart of this technological controversy.

Implants, which could carry every conceivable bit of information about the carrier, might provide an amicable solution to the struggle between the gun lobby and police agencies that are pushing for a waiting period before someone is permitted to buy a gun.

With the person's complete history, including criminal records, always on (in?) the person, gun dealers could immediately verify police-required security checks. This would eliminate the waiting period which gun lobbyists so ardently oppose. Of course, it is unlikely that the gun control dispute would be settled by this one piece of technology. But it might lead to gun-control measures that even the National Rifle Association—the largest gun lobby— would not consider a breach of personal freedoms.

Personal freedom and individual privacy are at the heart of this technological controversy. The American Civil Liberties Union is an ardent and extreme advocate of personal freedoms and privacy. But even one of its representatives from Florida, speaking about this implant technology, said that he would have no worries about such a device as long as individuals agreed to have it implanted. But he cautioned, "Somebody's bound to abuse it."[12]

Better Access to Medical Records

What would happen if your child were rushed to the hospital and you weren't there to approve treatment?

The Tag Team is a children's health and safety program, utilizing laminated tags that are worn by children on their shoe-laces or on necklaces, and cards that are carried in a wallet or left with a caregiver. Tag Team tags and cards contain the child's medical history and identification form reduced to microfilm. Information on how to immediately reach parents, relatives, family physicians and other contacts are provided on the microfilm. There is also an optional consent form which parents may sign to authorize emergency treatment.[13]

When accidents or sudden illnesses strike and the victim cannot communicate, it is not always easy or even possible to locate a medical card. An easily located card could contain vital information needed by emergency medical personnel. The card would most likely include vital information about allergic reactions to certain medicines and existing conditions that might preclude certain types of treatment.

In situations where every second counts, a good case can be made for implants. Emergency technicians wouldn't have to search a victim's wallet or purse or car for the medical card. The problems wouldn't be compounded because someone left the card at home.

Every ambulance, police car, and other emergency vehicle would be equipped with hand-held scanners that could read the implant immediately. Not only would this assist the professionals on the scene, but the information could be relayed to the resident doctor at the nearest available hospital.

Having knowledge of a victim's complete medical history before he arrives at the emergency room could greatly aid in diagnosing the extent of injuries and the best method of treatment. It could be the difference between life and death.

> *By its very nature, a system built to monitor all of the world's animals is a de facto test for a system capable of doing the same thing with people!*

To this point we've discussed only the societal issues that could be addressed by using implant technology. But did you know implant technology is already undergoing widespread testing and use in the animal kingdom?

Testing Implants in the Lab—Your Black Lab, That Is

Successful experiments with animals have propelled the microchip implant to the top of the list of electronic identity verifiers. Let's look at how the procedure has been successfully used in animals.

Koi, exotic members of the carp family valued at between $100 and $3,000 each, were disappearing from a public pond in California. When it was determined that the fish were being stolen rather than being eaten by herons or raccoons, a method of catching the thief had to be devised. Police believed they knew who the thief was (he had a koi pond of his own), but they needed proof of his larcenous activities.

"A veterinarian then implanted rice-grain-sized computer chips in the bellies of the fish. The carp can be identified by signals transmitted from the chips to an electronic wand," said H. L. Stoddard of American Veterinarian Identification Devices.[14]

A trip to the thief's pond with the electronic wand solved the problem on the spot. But such uses are only the tip of the iceberg. When cat lovers expressed concern about the danger of identification tags for their pets, innovators had a solution in mind.

If you refuse to allow your cat to wear an identification collar because of the possibility the collar might get caught on something and hang the cat, you might be interested in this new method of Identification Devices, Inc.... It's an ultra thin microchip, which a veterinarian will inject under the cat's skin.

The microchip emits a numerical or letter combination code (about 34 billion are possible), which is assigned exclusively to that cat. . . . Its inventors believe that the widespread use of this technique of permanent identification could help save some of the thousands of animals euthanized each year by shelters that cannot trace the cat's owners.[15]

At the same time, animal rights activists should be pleased with the following humane advance in technology:

Hot-iron branding of cattle in Canada may soon give way to a cool system of electronic identification.

Anitech Enterprises Inc. of Markham said Agriculture Canada has approved commercial introduction of the company's implantable electronic identification technology for cattle.

The approval was based on the results of combined field trials conducted over the past year by the company and the Holstein Association of Canada, Anitech said in a news release.

With government approval, Anitech said it has been able to begin its electronic ID program in the Canadian dairy ministry.[16]

Canada is not alone. The European Community's Executive Commission has passed legislation requiring that all livestock owned by EC farmers be implanted with microchips. Home pets also are being electronically identified by implants, and laboratory animals are not overlooked. Bio Medic Data Systems is a provider of this type of service:

> Nobody knows lab animal identification better than we do. Our unique Electronic Laboratory Animal Monitoring System (ELAMS) uses a miniature transponder implant and advanced microprocessor technology. It can link any animal to any computer database, allowing you to individualize your animal using your study number. Simply put it replaces the complexities and inaccuracies of toe clipping, ear tagging and tattooing with a foolproof, fast and economical method of positive identification.[17]

In Colorado Springs and dozens of other cities across North America, microchips have replaced dog tags. For $45 the Humane Society will implant the chip under the skin of the dog's neck. If picked up by the dogcatcher, a wand-like scanner will be used to read the chip and identify the owner.[18]

> From now on, identifying a pet adopted from county shelters will be *as easy as scanning a price tag at the supermarket*.

> Hector Cazares, acting director of the county Animal Control Department, said

Friday that all pets adopted from the shelters . . . will be entered into an electronic identification system.

A microchip transponder the size of a rice grain is injected under the pet's skin, usually behind the nape of the neck. An electronic scanner picks up the microchip's signal, which transmits an identification number used to look up the *pet's name, owner, birth date, medical records and other details contained in a computer database.*[19]

This pet-tracking technology is not optional in some parts of the world. In Spain, Big Brother is watching the pets.

Dogs and cats in Spain's largest cities must now undergo microchip implants to make it easier for authorities to reunite lost pets with their owners and track down those who'd rather abandon their animals than pay a sitter.

Four of Spain's 17 regions now require dog and cat owners to identify their pets with the chips or tattoos—apparently the only such laws in western Europe or North America.

"The whole object is not only to make it nationwide, but also Europe-wide and then universal," said Dr. William Hutchinson, a Scottish veterinarian working in Madrid [emphasis added].[20]

The natural transition from well-intentioned and voluntary participation to mandatory compliance should not escape our attention. But there's something even more significant here.

We are witnessing the development of an international, microchip-based system capable of tracking every animal on the face of the earth. By its very nature, a system built to monitor all of the world's animals is a de facto test for a system capable of doing the same thing with people!

In fact, Identification Devices, Inc., a leader in the field, made the scope of their plans clear in a recent promotional flyer:

> Suppose you were to make a list of the technical advances that are quickly reshaping the way we live: microminiaturization of electronic components, high speed data processing systems, powerful new computer programming techniques and extremely sophisticated telecommunication devices. . . . Then consider how these innovations might be employed to solve the age old problem of providing positive identification of *people*, animals and equipment [emphasis added].[21]

In the Right Hand or Forehead

Let us say it very clearly. What we are describing is *not* the mark of the beast, yet it *is* a tremendous proof of the accuracy of God's Word. Almost 2,000 years since the prophecy was uttered, we are witnessing the birth of a cashless society and the ever-expanding use of microchip implants to track animals all over the world—a likely precursor to the antichrist's worldwide monitoring system of *people*.

One thing is for sure. For the first time in history, the technology to easily fulfill this incredible prophecy exists. Let's now turn our attention to another aspect of this prophecy, which begins with the words "and he causeth..."

6

||||||

If You're Not Paranoid, It's Because You're Not Paying Close Enough Attention!

Gospel singer Dan Smith wrote a song called "God's Radar Is Fixed on You." It's comforting to Christians that God not only knows who they are, but where they are and what they're going through.

A similar capability by a not-so-benevolent source, however, should cause us concern. As we are about to see, the equipment to track every person on the earth and monitor most of their activities already has been developed. More chillingly, most of it is already operational!

But before we look at these tracking systems, let's review what we've already learned. We know that if we use a plastic card such as a credit card, we will get a statement at the end of the month telling us how much we owe the card company. But there is more to it than that. To verify our charges, the statement lists every purchase we've made and where we made it. More than one husband's secret purchase of new golf clubs has been discovered because of this technology.

> *The equipment to track every person on the earth and monitor most of their activities already has been developed.*

Even today, if we used our card for every purchase we made during a month, the card company could recreate just about everywhere we went and when we were there. In a cashless society where you had no choice but to conduct your business electronically, such tracking capabilities would be dramatically increased.

Now add to that some of the items discussed in other portions of this book and consider what it might mean to something like international travel. As the global community has opened up, business travel between countries has increased greatly. Nowhere is this more true than within the European Community. To speed the process, automatic customs turnstiles are being developed. The busy traveler need only insert his or her smart card into the terminal and let the electronic device take a quick fingerprint reading to verify personal identity. In a flash he has cleared customs and filled in another blank on his activities log for the keepers of the database.

Now the picture becomes a little clearer. In an electronic society, every bit of information is captured and stored in giant databases. While a cash purchase is nearly untraceable, an electronic one is recorded forever. The potential for abuse is staggering.

> Every credit card purchase casts a shadow. So does each entry into a security-minded workplace or store, application for health insurance, call to a phone sex service, selection of a pay-per-view movie or movement of a cellular telephone.

> It's called a data shadow, and it grows longer as computer databases record more and more of our daily activities. The image reveals who we are, where we go, whom we know, what we do and when—sort of an electronic alter ego that is required for us to obtain credit, receive welfare benefits, vote, get a job or cross a border without a hassle.

> *The global village is fast growing into surveillance city.*[1]

Despite these incredible dangers, society is caught in a "technological trance," according to Canadian Privacy Commissioner Bruce Phillips. He declared in his latest report that information—any information—is for sale to the highest bidder! At a recent "This Week in Bible Prophecy" conference, a notary gave us a copy of her profession's national magazine, *The National Notary*. The magazine stated that there is no longer any fear of where we are heading: "Arguments raising the cry of 'invasion of privacy' are antiquated and almost date the loudest proponents as stuck in the last century."[2]

Despite this lack of concern, the Bible's warning is very clear. We musn't forget that the prophecy concerning the mark of the beast begins with the words, "And he causeth all . . ." If you are going to *cause* anyone to do anything, there has to be some teeth in your bite.

This is what the Bible is trying to tell us about the antichrist system. While it will be desirable to most of the world, those who do not submit will be systematically excluded from almost every activity. There will be virtually no way to function outside of the system.

So how far have we come? Let us answer that by describing some of the leading-edge technologies of our day. Then judge for yourself. As we sketch out some of these systems, take note of the good and desirable reasons given for their introduction. It almost makes you forget that the price of these tremendous breakthroughs is your very freedom.

Electronic Tracking Promoted by Crimebusters

Automobile theft has been increasing about 15 percent a year for the past ten years and is now an eight-billion-dollar-a-year business. Police say that 80 percent of the cars are stolen by professional car thieves, not by joyriders or first-timers.[3]

Tracking systems already available are being touted by police departments as a real deterrent in the battle against car thieves. At least two companies, Teletrak and LoJack, are now making these antitheft devices. They cost between $500 and $900 installed, but police, insurers, and car owners say they are worth it. Both companies say they recover about 95 percent of the stolen cars that are equipped with the systems.[4]

Here's how these locator systems work: A transmitter about the size of a videocassette tape or a chalkboard eraser is hidden in the vehicle. In the Teletrak system, when a thief starts the car without disarming the system, the unit begins to send out a signal that is tracked on an electronic map. The LoJack system, on the other hand, must be activated by the owner once he realizes his car has been stolen. Either way, the police can now electronically follow the stolen car.

Car 54, Where Are You?

These vehicle locator systems are not available everywhere, but everyone seems pleased with the results where the systems have been implemented.

A LoJack representative said that of 200,000 cars equipped with its system, 4,500 have been stolen and 95 percent of those have been recovered.

In France, a similar system has been developed for nationwide use. A writer for *The European* tells us about it:

> The James Bond-style tracking device that distraught car-theft victims have always dreamed of can now finally be theirs. A computer chip available to French motorists for installation in their cars will alert police to its location anywhere in the country—should it ever have the misfortune of being driven away illegally.
>
> The device is a revolution in the war against car crime, now at epidemic levels throughout Europe.... When the system goes live, an electronic trip wire will stretch the length and breadth of France, enabling monitors in a control center to fix a "hot" car's position as it crosses its beam. Eventually, say the system's backers, there is no reason why the network should not extend across the continent.[5]

An Ominous Prospect

Arno Froese of Midnight Call Ministries, whom we quoted earlier, points out the clear connection of these tests to end-time events.

During 1991, over 270,000 cars were stolen in France alone. Any device that will discourage theft can only be welcomed. Of course, the effect will be good only until the thief finds the computer chip and removes it. However, inventors will not cease to create the undetectable device that cannot be removed. Thus, our thoughts are guided to the time when man too will come under the control of the electronic beast that will lead to the fulfillment of Revelation 13:17: "... that no man might buy or sell, save he that had the mark, or the name of the beast, or the number of his name."[6]

But Boss, Joe's the Slacker

What are some other uses being promoted for these tracking devices? In England, a company has developed a clip-on microcomputer identification badge which makes it easy to locate employees who have to move from location to location in a large office complex. It is also being tried in hospitals in order to keep in constant touch with patients and doctors.

New York Times writer Leonard Sloane provides this ominous lead to his story on the intelligent badge:

> Another tool that lets "them" check up on "us"—where we are and with whom we are—is on the way. It is the active badge,

a small clip-on microcomputer about the size of an employee ID card, that transmits signals to a central system. As long as you wear the badge, the system can track your movements around an office building or even a larger area.[7]

Scientists found that with a badge emitting an identification code every 15 seconds to a network of wall-mounted sensors around a building, information about the location of the person wearing it could be constantly updated.

Global Positioning Systems

Of course, today's technologies make tracking people within a hospital seem insignificant. For example, the world was introduced to the Global Positioning System during round-the-clock television coverage of the Gulf War in 1991. Soldiers carried small hand-held computerized units whose exact location was monitored by satellites high above the desert. The satellites in this high-tech network enabled U.S. forces to find the right way through and around unmapped sand dunes to arrive at their prescribed destination. *The Economist* magazine discussed the success of this system:

> Having seen its success, the American forces [busily equipped] everything, from battleships to cruise missiles, with GPS systems. The technology may have as many

applications in peace as in war—or even more.[8]

New high-tech companies, along with old-line tech firms, are looking for civilian markets for this unique system. There is a huge potential market for machines with the ability to tell exactly where a thing or a person is, at any time.

The Economist article said that Sony has developed a hand-held device costing a few hundred dollars which will enable a user to tell, within a hundred meters, his or her exact latitude and longitude. Panasonic has developed one with a larger price tag ($1,195), but with much more accuracy. By linking computer and satellite, the device can display the wearer's global position within three meters.[9]

More Military Intelligence

The military has long been in the forefront of such tracking technology. To speed the processing of personnel and supplies, for example, the U.S. Department of Defense has married bar codes and smart cards with personal computers and portable readers.

Using smart cards to identify key personnel and bar codes to identify critical cargo, the system greatly accelerates mobilization. The Air Force has found that the Automated Mobility Processing System (AMPS) not only saves time, it saves dollars. Recall messages that used to take 5.5 hours to prepare now take just 16 minutes by using AMPS.

Per-man costs were cut from $69 to just $3.[10] These impressive results are possible by pinpointing the exact location of men and equipment at any time during a rapid deployment. John Dunbar, a reporter for the *Fairborne Daily Herald*, described how the system works after he witnessed a demonstration at Wright-Patterson Air Force Base in Ohio:

> Thursday's demonstration worked on the assumption that a civil engineering unit was needed overseas for rapid runway repair. In this case, the scenario was the unit was to be sent to Germany, although the same system would be used for a deployment to Saudi Arabia.
>
> The 125-member unit was dispatched to the mobility processing center on base, and unit members checked in by using individual computer cards which are read with hand-held computers, much like a grocery store bar code reader.
>
> The computer checks a soldier against a list of personnel who should be reporting for departure. A second card reader then checks a soldier's immunization. The final application for the system is for when a soldier actually gets on an airplane to deploy. His or her card serves as a boarding pass to check the unit's muster.[11]

This highly successful pilot program will probably mean that units in all branches of the military will be using the AMPS system soon. Ultimately, it means that the U.S. government will enjoy constant electronic confirmation of the location of every person in the armed forces!

Sometimes I Think the Car Knows Its Own Way to the Golf Course

Much of what we have so far described does not immediately affect the average man or woman. So why should anyone be concerned?

Here's why: It is inevitable that a major portion of the population will soon be involved with one of these systems. Perhaps the most fascinating—and most likely to realize widespread implementation soon—are "smart" travel systems.

Travelers won't have to try to remember directions or scribble them on scraps of paper. Family feuds that spoil many vacations (because dad won't ask directions when he gets lost) will be a thing of the past when cars are equipped with the new Trav-Tek navigational system.

This is still an experimental system, but it may be universally available in just a few years. "Smart" cars are equipped with a microcomputer and a dash-mounted color video screen that displays navigation maps and information on area attractions, hotels, restaurants, and special events. One reporter described her experience with a car like this:

It could have been a scene from a Jetsons cartoon. As the passengers climbed in the Oldsmobile Toronado the destination was keyed into the vehicle's computer.

The driver pulled away from the curb. A short way down the road, the car computer announced, "Take a left onto Landerson Street." As long as the driver followed the directions of the car, there was no way to get lost. The car's computer had the route plotted. [12]

It is estimated that the device, when available to the public, will cost less than $1,000. The American Automobile Association, General Motors Corporation, and the Federal Highway Administration have been jointly developing the TravTec system.

As interesting as this is, it's only the beginning. Systems are being developed to improve traffic flows in metropolitan areas and collect tolls from commuters without slowing them down (much less stopping them) at a traffic-jamming toll booth.

New York City, for example, has been considering charging tolls on all bridges that cross the East and Harlem Rivers into Manhattan. The main reason for hesitating has been the nightmarish traffic jams that would result. Opponents also have cited increased concentrations of automobile pollution. [13]

Technology once again may provide an answer to the dilemma. Electronic scanners which read toll tags mounted on windshields as the cars whiz by will eliminate the main nonmonetary complaints about the proposed tolls.

Scanner systems already exist that can read data on a microchip as it passes through a reader beam at a hundred miles an hour. As a chip-equipped vehicle passes the collection point, the scanner reads the chip and automatically deducts the toll from the account of the owner. Such a system would not only speed up toll collection, but would reduce costs and pollution, increase safety (by eliminating a lot of stopping on the high-speed toll roads and by reducing risks as drivers fumble for change), and improve efficiency at collection points.

Honey, I Told You That You Were Driving Too Fast Last Week

As a side benefit, the systems may increase revenue in another way. Scanners can record a vehicle's speed, activate a citation-issuing process, and collect traffic fines. Already there are many test sites across North America where you might just receive a traffic ticket in the mail.

There are also countless tests being run where the microchip on your smart card can be read by the system as you pass through, without requiring you to take the card out of your wallet. The system simply accesses your card by a radio frequency, confirms that you are indeed supposed to pass through security, records your entrance, and moves on to the next person. You never even know that it has taken place.

In the implant world of the future, you wouldn't need a microchip on your windshield. Your personal microchip could just as easily be activated as you pass through a toll. No additional equipment would have to be added to the vehicle for the system to work. Amazing, isn't it?

Highways with IQs Higher Than Those of Some Drivers

AT&T has reached an agreement with Lockheed to develop Intelligent Vehicle Highway Systems (IVHS) that may be a 200-billion-dollar business over the next 20 years in the United States alone.[14] The catalyst for this bold undertaking was statistics from the General Accounting Office which estimate that traffic congestion wastes two billion gallons of fuel annually and causes productivity losses of about $100 million each year.[15]

Monday morning, and you hop into your car for the daily commute to work. You start the engine and a video map display lights up, showing you the quickest route. As you move through the suburban streets to the freeway, a computer voice advises: "Stay in this lane and prepare to take the second right. Continue at 55 mph. You reach the interstate and ease into the traffic flow. Glancing out your window, *you can't see them, but you have total confidence that the sensors along the freeway will keep you a safe distance from the cars in front and behind.* You move easily through the specially designed automatic vehicle identification toll lanes without stopping, since appropriate

fees are automatically processed for convenient payment.[16]

Alan Smith, a GM executive vice president,
notes that technology is not the issue: "While we are
testing the technical systems, we are particularly
interested in the human-side factor of the project.
We want to see how customers react to and use the
equipment."[17]

The U.S. smart-highway projects may
seem impressive, but they are minuscule
compared to projects in Japan and Europe.
In Japan, an onboard navigation system is
being tested in a Tokyo-based pilot study
sponsored by the Japanese government
and 50 automotive and electronics companies. A colorful map of Tokyo appears on
a computer screen near the driver's seat.
With a touch of a button, the map zooms in
to cover a chosen area and a yellow triangle
traces the car's movements across the map.

In Europe five governments, 14 automotive tire companies and 70 corporate
and electronics firms are collaborating on
the world's most ambitious smart highway
project, an eight year, billion dollar experiment called Prometheus. [Soon] Munich,
Seville, Paris, Toulouse and Turin will all
be experimenting with the smart highway
system.[18]

The United States has no choice but to catch up.
Estimates are that the average speed on California's

crammed freeways will be only 11 miles per hour in the year 2000. IVHS, when implemented, is expected to reduce commuting time by 50 percent and reduce emissions by 15 percent.[19] *Card Technology Today* reveals more details of the American effort:

> AT&T's experience in electronic toll collection goes back several years to its initial collaboration with Olivetti in developing a payment system where vehicles could pay tolls without having to stop at a toll plaza. Since 1991, the company has also been working with Vapor Canada on developing smart card based toll collection techniques. Outside the smart card field, the company is also working on a system to monitor traffic flow via the transmission of video pictures from the roadside, and is involved in linking speech recognition and synthesis into traveler information services. Peter Skarzynski, managing director of AT&T's IVHS Communications Systems, is reported as saying that, "Pouring concrete is no longer the best answer to our traffic problems. We should be making our roads smarter, not wider. Having assigned $659 million over six years for the development of IVHS systems, it seems that the U.S. government may well agree."[20]

The plain fact is that as good as these systems will be at speeding up traffic and streamlining toll collections, they also have a very real side effect.

The government will have the ability to know exactly where you are at any point in time. While we do not claim that this is the goal of such a system, there is little doubt that in the hands of a totalitarian government, such a system presents a huge potential for control. From a prophetic point of view, we are undoubtedly watching the guts of the antichrist system coming into place.

Even the Cattle on Your Field Are Numbered

Here's another interesting tidbit. While parcels of land don't move around, the European Community nevertheless is keeping close tabs on farm plots. *The European* details the EC spy in the sky:

> Brussels has launched spy satellite surveillance of Europe's nine million farmers in the intensifying war against fraud. In all but two of the 12 member states, the fields of thousands of farmers who make bogus claims for hefty EC subsidies are being detected with pinpoint accuracy.
>
> For the first time, satellite surveillance makes it possible to carry out checks on virtually every farm, largely superseding the cumbersome procedure of random on-the-spot checks by agriculture ministry officials.
>
> In Brussels, the Commission is collating the spy satellite data, then passing it on

to national enforcement agencies in readiness for a blitz on fraudsters once the autumn harvest begins.

The first task for EC experts is to give every field a serial number and identify the type of crop being grown. Detailed analysis can then reveal whether the actual plot tallies with a farmer's application for subsidy.

The Commission's response has been ambitious. They have invested Ecu 115 million in a scheme centralizing records on who farms what. A "Domesday Book" (sic) would be compiled listing every field and animal across Europe. It would be policed by satellite surveillance and a new electronic system of tagging livestock.[21]

Tracking and tagging livestock seems almost bizarre, even to prevent fraud. But remember, if the antichrist is going to control all commerce and all buying and selling, he would have to control bartering. A cow traded for vegetables might elude the electronic accounting system—but not the "sky spy" that counts and tracks livestock and brussels sprouts.

No Man Might Buy or Sell

Remember that any electronic activity can easily be recorded and stored in a giant database. Then consider the following few examples of how widespread the tracking system is becoming:

- The Chicago area has an off-line point of service (just like point of sale) system that uses smart cards as an "electronic purse" for disabled persons who take advantage of paratransit services.

- The State of Wyoming uses smart cards to distribute electronic welfare benefits, enabling the state to regulate the items welfare clients are allowed to buy and to limit the quantities that can be sold by merchants in the system.

- The U.S. Department of Agriculture uses more than 200,000 smart cards to regulate marketing, reconcile inventory, and record payments in its Peanut Buying Point Automation System. It has been in successful operation since 1987.

- Orange County, California, already has three new roads that collect tolls from cars passing at full speed. The same system is in use in Italy and France.

An Olivetti lab in Cambridge, England, has gone a step further. It has linked its computer badge (worn by employees) to a global electronic mail network, so that people can find out where an employee is, provided they know his or her electronic mail address.[22]

At the same time, according to a government report, claims that "computers that can monitor rest breaks and productivity, sometimes by counting individual keystrokes, are keeping track of more than seven million American workers."[23] Kmart is using computers on the sales floor in an experiment to track customers as they shop. According to David M. Carlson, senior vice-president of Corporate Information Systems, "Customers won't even know that ShopperTrak is there." They will use the system to learn not only how many people shop in a store, but where the store needs more clerks and when it should open more checkouts.

Technology exists today that can easily track the movements and activities of every citizen. A government that can do this can control its people.

The point should be clear: The technology exists, right now, to track the movements of an entire society, an entire world! All that is required is for the system to be codified, unified, and established according to emerging industry standards.

Big Brother May Not Be Watching, But He Could If He Wanted to!

Technology exists today that can easily track the movements and activities of every citizen. A government that can do this can control its people. Skeptics scoff at the idea we are in the last days and that this may be the generation spoken of in the book of Revelation. They doubt that this is the first generation fully capable of being the last generation.

But it is sobering to think about what the government already is capable of. Resistance by watchdog groups is waning. So much information about every citizen is already in databases—it seems pointless, many say, to resist. Soon, those people who are not cooperating can expect to have their "electronic purse" turned off. They will be incapable of conducting even the most mundane business dealing. All assemblies can be detected, infiltrated, and identified. Hiding will be impossible. How can you hide when even the highways are watching you?

And remember what Terry Galanoy, the former director of communications for (what is now) Visa has said:

> Protesting too loudly about it isn't going to help either, because the disturbance you kick up is going to end up in one of your files. And on that come-and-get-it day when we're totally and completely dependent upon our card—*or whatever security device might replace it*—you might be left all alone without one.[24]

Fortunately, for the student of Bible prophecy, a different future awaits.

7

Bringing the World On-Line

As astonishing as these technologies are, the coming man of sin, or antichrist, cannot fully control the buying and selling of the entire world until these technologies are pulled together into an integrated network with common, universal standards. He could not control even the conduct of business between two independent countries if they continued to use different card technologies, computer software, and tracking systems.

Today, however, international networking and the establishment of global industry standards are quickly putting this problem well into the rearview mirror. Governments and other institutions are expanding their electronic networking by sharing information, services, and technology. Proponents of these cooperative efforts always point out the positive aspects, such as lowered costs and improved efficiency in the delivery of goods or services. Little is ever said about the negative aspects of governmental or commercial intrusion into the previously private affairs of individuals.

As we've already noted, few people are still afraid of Big Brother. They succumb to cleverly devised marketing strategies that, to quote Tigger in *Jungle Book*, "accentuate the positive and eliminate the negative."

Your PC—Going On-Line with the New World Order

In this chapter, we want to look at this networking. It involves various levels of government, private business, the banking industry, and all of the major players in the global communications industry. In time, we will see the private sector and the government combining their resources and technologies to further control and track people's activities—all, of course, in the name of cost-effectiveness and personal service.

Revelation 13 tells us that, in the coming new world order, there will be a global economic system where all business transactions can be traced. As we have demonstrated, computer technology probably will be central to this system.

At the individual level, in recent years we have witnessed the birth of concepts like home shopping and banking via personal computers. Even a decade ago we heard how we were on the verge of seeing every home equipped with a personal computer, without which you could barely survive. But this vision has been slow in coming to reality. Public resistance, not the technology, has been the stick in the spokes.

Your TV Is Tuning In

Jeffrey Zygmont, writing in *Omni* magazine, says:

> It looks as if the techno-marketeers may reach their elusive goal at last to put a computer in every American home. We might all succumb this time because the computer is cleverly disguised to look like a television.[1]

Zygmont also wrote that when computers were still new, marketing experts were limited in the scope of their vision, envisioning these home terminals only for balancing checkbooks and storing recipes. In that light, he argues, it is...

> no wonder they fell miserably short of their wish to put a computer in every home. Nintendo has come much closer, selling nearly 30 million game systems since the early eighties. But then, Nintendo distills what people seem to want most from computers in their leisure: fun.[2]

This still does not represent how far we have come. TVs are about to become two-way devices through what is known as interactive television, which planners say will "transform TV from a passive spectator-deadening device into a truly interactive tool, one that prods you to interact as well with the real world."[3]

People are so accustomed to and comfortable with television that their fears of computers and Big Brother are assuaged by integrating computer technology with their very familiar television set. Even the government is aiding in this technological transformation:

> The Federal Communications Commission paved the way for the proliferation of a technology that permits TV owners to bank, pay bills and order everything from Chinese food to tennis shoes through the boob-tube. A remote control device accesses menu screens offering up the various services.
>
> The product of Virginia-based TV Answer Inc., interactive television transmits data via radio waves to a base station linked by satellite to the firm's headquarters. The systems will be available in 25 major cities by the end of the year.[4]

This anecdote illustrates how a privately owned, high-tech company can network with banks, restaurants, and retail stores to provide customers with better service—and, of course, have the blessing of the government in doing so. Don't forget, however, that to conduct your affairs electronically is to have your personal business entered into the system—a system that never forgets.

Merging Data and Banks

The information age which unofficially began in the late 1970s has been overtaken by a new age, according to a U.S. Department of Justice study. The new period is being dubbed the *"electronic information age."*

Here's how the Information Commission of Canada reported on this new development:

> One estimate has it that within the next decade, nearly 80 percent of all public sector information will be fully digital.

> On-line databases, that is computer-held information which can be electronically transferred from one computer to another, have expanded at a breathtaking rate. In 1980, the number of these databases worldwide was 400; at the end of 1990, there were 4,615. Sellers of on-line services have grown from 59 to 654 during the same period.

> The money statistics are perhaps even more impressive. The authoritative study of the Link Resources Corporation . . . reports:

> > The total electronic information revenues in North America alone were

$6.551 billion (U.S.) in 1988 and are forecast to reach $19.784 billion by 1994—tripling in six years![5]

Information on the purchases or the whereabouts of an individual can be transferred between these databases in milliseconds, although they're thousands of miles apart. This is essential in a world where a central authority is able to track the buying and selling of every person on the face of the earth.

Thailand: On the Cutting Edge

The government of Thailand has been honored for being the hero of this electronic information age. Although a relative novice to the world of computers, the Thai government has made tremendous progress in showing the rest of the world how to network a large number of varied social services. Under the headline "Peddling Big Brother," *Time* magazine detailed the Thai success.

Technocrats may admire systems like Bangkok's, which by 2006 will have stored vital data on 65 million Thais in a single, integrated computer network. At first glance the Thai system, which is being considered for possible adoption by Indonesia and the Philippines, seems harmless enough. Every citizen over age 15 will be required to carry a card bearing a color photo, various pertinent facts and an identification number.

But behind the cards are a $50 million computer system and sophisticated software that could enable a Big Brother government to create a dossier quickly that would tell it just about anything it wanted to know about anybody. The program, which runs on three top-of-the-line Control Data mainframes, is known as a relational database, and it permits bureaucrats to correlate the files of otherwise disparate government offices.

If the necessary links to the revenue and police departments are put in place, a few key taps could cross-reference criminal records to tax records to *religious and family information* in order to draw a startlingly detailed description of any individual or group [emphasis added].[6]

More Than the Sum of Its Parts

Many countries throughout the world are availing themselves of the latest technologies to solve their peculiar social, economic, and military problems. As they become more adept at using the technology, they too will expand its capabilities and its reaches. There is no doubt that the time is coming soon when these national and regional systems will join the global age. Although the level of technological development varies from nation to nation, the whole system could be "on line" in a short time.

Unfortunately, little thought is being given to the dire consequences that are possible. Nor is any thought being given to the biblical warnings about the one world government that will soon spring upon the scene. Under the banner of science and expanded human wisdom, the governments of the world rush to complete the kind of system the Bible so specifically warns about.

Building the Global Infrastructure

Of course, there would be no global electronic infrastructure if there were not a new international economic order to build it upon. With the birth of multinational corporations, the world bank, the G7, the Gatt, and the International Monetary Fund, there is no doubt that we have entered the global economic age. You have only to witness how a crash in the New York Stock Exchange is immediately felt in Tokyo, London, and Bonn to see how economically interconnected we have become.

Although the level of technological development varies from nation to nation, the whole system could be "on line" in a short time.

The banking scandal involving the Bank of

Credit and Commerce International (BCCI) propelled to the forefront efforts to improve supervision of banking operations on a worldwide scale. Here's how the Reuter News Service covered this development:

> BCCI, indicted in New York last week on charges of fraud, theft and money laundering, escaped close scrutiny in the more than 70 countries where it operated, because no single country was responsible for overseeing all of its operations, banking regulators said.
>
> U.S. Federal Deposit Insurance Corp. chairman William Seidman said that the BCCI scandal overscored the need for global co-operation on bank regulation. *"We will need a supervisory system at the world level that will be capable of handling supervision of banks that operate in many countries around the world,"* he said.[7]

If such a supervisory structure comes into being, it not only will be able to closely regulate the activities of the banks themselves, but also will have instant access to information about individual accounts. It seems a dangerous thing to allow one entity such access to personal account records, but there is probably no preventing it.

And did you notice that the alleged criminal activities of BCCI were the impetus for this talk of a new regulatory agency? Isn't it curious that improprieties by banks are the reason given for creating a global "superbank," run by these same bankers?

Nonetheless, crime-stopping is a prime motivator in much of this new technology and the resultant networking of various organizations and systems. Here's another example, as explained by Joseph Battaglia.

> As with so many things the government does, the process of attacking the free economy has been a gradual one. It began with the introduction of so-called anti-money-laundering rules. These rules required banks and businesses to report to the IRS (Internal Revenue Service) the name, address and social security number of individuals who engage in cash transactions of $10,000 or more. This rule was established under the guise of attacking drug dealers. With the tremendous publicity given to the drug problem and so-called "money-laundering," the government was able to obtain this repressive, anti-freedom, money-laundering law.[8]

Battaglia further says that a Money Laundering Enforcement Conference was sponsored by the American Bankers Association and the American Bar Association and was attended by representatives of several federal law enforcement agencies. "Together," Battaglia says, "they comprise the financial enforcement arm of the New World Order."[9]

Battaglia's gloomy prognostication may be a little exaggerated—it is doubtful a network of strictly U.S. agencies could enforce monetary policies on a global scale—but he rightly points to this development as a harbinger of the erosion of personal freedom and privacy.

The *McAlvany Intelligence Advisor* also sees a soon-coming day when the electronic capabilities of this generation will be used to track every single transaction:

> The Financial Criminal Enforcement Network (FINCEN) said that *"we currently have nearly all financial information available on every U.S. citizen."* In the future, tax violations will be treated as money laundering violations. (Reread that sentence!) This and other measures discussed at the meeting will wipe out virtually all vestiges of financial freedom and privacy for the American people.[10]

And America is just the beginning, according to McAlvany. In the name of fighting crime, laws are being passed or proposed on a global level unthinkable in other generations.

The Bible clearly links the global mark-of-the-beast system with the emergence of a global world order.

First there was the United Nations money laundering treaty, which attempts to outlaw bank secrecy. (The U.N. Treaty, to which America is a signatory, criminalizes international money laundering, allows seizure of assets, attempts to destroy all bank secrecy laws, and weakens protections involved in the production of evidence, the taking of testimony, and the extradition of offenders.) Then the 12-nation tax treaty of the Organization for Economic Cooperation and Development was ratified to ensure cooperation in harassing taxpayers.

Most recently we have a report from the Research Institute for the Study of Conflict and Terrorism (which works closely with the CIA) which argues that global money laundering is not just the $500 billion it is normally estimated to be, but two to three times that large. The report blames the lack of CTR regulations in most countries besides the U.S. and says that Swiss, Austrian, Hong Kong and Caribbean bank secrecy must be destroyed immediately.[11]

At about the time that article appeared, *USA Today* reported that:

Switzerland is abolishing most of its anonymous bank accounts to crack down on criminal transactions. [The] country's Federal Banking Commission will demand that bank account holders identify themselves, thereby making it difficult for drug runners and dictators to launder money.[12]

These few examples clearly point to the piece-meal, backdoor way a global system is being established that wipes out any secrecy in our private financial affairs. But the drive toward a global economic system is being pushed on a very public front as well. Recently, U.S. President Clinton has made clear the administration's view by his all-out push for NAFTA—the North American Free Trade Agreement.

> This new global economy is here to stay. We can't wish it away. We can't run from it. We can't build walls around our nation. So we must provide world leadership, we must compete, not retreat.[13]

Abba Eban, former Israeli foreign minister, says the G7 partners (seven of the richest Western nations) could be a real force for action, but...

> They have not learned to think together. They bring together extraordinary concentration of power, but their meetings don't seem to produce anything. They should recognize that collectively they have immense power to change the human condition, but individually they do not. They should set up a *permanent institution, almost like a new state*. Existing bodies cannot do the job. That would require both the wisdom and the leadership qualities of *modern-day philosopher-kings*. Though there may be some waiting in the wings, none seem to be stalking the stage now.[14]

The Revived Roman Empire

Scripture clearly shows that a new world order will create a global society which will blossom out of Western democracies in general and Western Europe in particular. In the beginning stages of European union that we are witnessing today, we would expect to see the emergence of many of the issues that will arise on the global level in the days ahead. And that is exactly what's happening. "Borderless Borders," a recent conference in Barcelona, Spain, was convened to deal with the problems of open borders. As you read the following portions of conference materials, keep in mind that the Bible clearly links the global mark-of-the-beast system with the emergence of a global world order.

Card technology applications are being affected radically by the dramatic changes in a Western Europe in the process of uniting with an emerging, new Eastern Europe. . . .

Issues which must be addressed include:

Identification: What information is necessary? Who are the keepers of the database? Will international passports be issued by individual nations or a central bureau, for example, in the European Community (EC)?

Security: How much identification is necessary to ensure a nation's security?

> Telecommunications: . . . Who will make the decisions—government, business or a worldwide entity?

> Banking/POS: Why should integrated Circuit/smart cards or debit cards replace cash? How much will identification and social service requirements drive these card applications?[15]

A system very like that described in Scripture—and perhaps the very one—is being openly discussed by world leaders. And the connection between this economic system and the new world order is unmistakable. Listen to Arlen Lessen, president of International Card Technology Institute:

> This is a very important conference—and not just because of the issues to be raised. The purpose of this conference is to formally and informally create a dialogue among the people who must make decisions about how we are going to live in an open world.

> We are not yet a global community. But that is clearly the direction in which we are heading. Borders will tend to blur and disappear on levels of economic, technological, political, military and even social activities. How can the integrity and security of a nation be maintained if people are free to cross from one nation to another? Of course, there must be some constraints,

some means of knowing who is wishing to cross, some means of monitoring and/or identifying people from various nations.[16]

Technologies like those we have been discussing will allow for this prophesied free flow of people, information, and commerce. Satellite and computer technology can quickly verify identifications and track individuals within three meters of their location anywhere on earth. The European Community is ready to implement such a borderless system among its members. It will no doubt create the pattern the rest of the world eventually will adopt.

Marking Those Intolerant Fundamentalists

We should stop here to clearly point out something. The Bible emphasizes that in the last days such a system will not only be in place to make possible the global order, but to make sure that anyone outside of the system cannot function. We know that anyone who serves God will be hated by this new world order of man!

It should come as no surprise, then, that the birth of the technology for the mark of the beast should have similar overtones. As we just quoted: "Of course, there must be some constraints, some means of knowing who is wishing to cross, some means of monitoring and/or identifying people from various nations."

> *The Bible emphasizes that in the last days such a system will not only be in place to make possible the global order, but to make sure that anyone outside of the system cannot function.*

We found it very interesting that when our research team attended the 1993 "Solutions for the Global Frontier" card technology conference in Washington, the United States was in the midst of the David Koresh disaster in Waco. Our researchers sat and watched with conference attendees as televisions all over the convention center showed the compound going up in flames.

Since the only electronic media at this conference were CNN and "This Week in Bible Prophecy," you can imagine how hard it was to get an interview after that! As He does so often, however, the Lord worked it out for good. The Waco debacle got the microchip experts talking about how their electronic identification systems could track religious cult members. One European leader told us flat out that Europe could keep these crazy American Christians out of Europe. To him, David Koresh was just another Christian! Not too long thereafter, the following appeared in *The European* newspaper:

STRASBOURG—A "directory" of religious cults looks likely to be approved by the Council of Europe in the wake of the Waco disaster in the United States, in which at least 80 sect members burnt to death this week. A report before the 26-nation council's committee of ministers voices concern over the activities of new religious cults. Member governments are asked to set up independent bodies to monitor and collect information, which should then be "widely circulated to the general public."

At the same time in France, the National Union of Associations for the Defense of the Family and the Individual issued just such a directory. Among the list of cults were the Full Gospel Businessmen's Fellowship International and the Assemblies of God!

Unfortunately, this is becoming a global identity crisis. The enemy is succeeding in getting the world to believe that all Christians are as imbalanced as the cult followers in Waco or Guyana. Listen to what *USA Today* said about identifying a cult in the aftermath of the Waco torching:

Today the groups tend to believe the Bible predicts the end of the world is near. . . . Such seemingly unrelated events as the Israelis' gaining control of Jerusalem in 1967, the threat of nuclear war and shifts in the global economy are among the signs *cult-ists* see that—as prophesied in the Bible—

the end is near and Jesus Christ will return.[17]

It is no coincidence that leaders in the field of electronic identification, microchips, and smart cards see how their technology can identify dangerous religious fanatics. They think they are protecting the world itself, and you can't help but note how accurately the scenario foretold in the Bible is coming to pass. No wonder the Scripture warns that "whosoever killeth you will think that he doeth God service" (John 16:2). While this text speaks of all generations, like everything else we can expect it to be amplified in the last generation. Today, Europe—the heart of tomorrow's world—sees the connection the Bible speaks of and is putting it into place. How close must we be?

8

||||||

666: The System Is Born

The account of the mark of the beast is one of the best-known prophecies in all of Scripture. Even most people who have never opened a Bible are familiar with the phrase and can sense the eeriness that accompanies the number *666*. Moviemakers in films such as *The Omen* and *The Exorcist* have used antichrist images, demonic activities, and 666 typology to introduce this idea to the world. Rock groups such as Iron Maiden have used it to terrify this last days generation. What is missing in so much of the secular (and often Christian) discussion of the mark of the beast is the context in which this prophecy is presented to us in the Scriptures. We would be remiss and poor biblical teachers if we were to concentrate on this one prophecy without showing how it dovetails with so many other prophecies.

The Bible says the mark of the beast and its accompanying technology will be installed by the antichrist—not as an end in itself, but as a means of managing the new world order that is even now being created. As intriguing as a discussion of the mark-of-the-beast technology may be, however, it does not attain its true significance until we put that piece of the puzzle into place with other pieces of the prophetic scenario.

It is crucial to understand that the decision to take the mark of the beast involves some form of a pledge of allegiance to the antichrist, making it a spiritual decision that has only secondary economic benefits.

The new world order will be a complex and complicated system to administer, even for a man who can perform great "lying signs and wonders." To track the movements of people, equipment, goods, and finances, it will take a sophisticated system much like the one we have described. It is just this sort of system—and perhaps this exact one—that will enable the coming world ruler to control the global government, the universal monetary system, and the unified religion that together will comprise the new world order.

A Global Pledge of Allegiance

When you consider that, according to the Scriptures, those who take the mark of the beast will be eternally damned, it becomes clear that the most important aspect of the mark is not economic but spiritual. Failure to understand this key point has often led to gross misinterpretations, a steady stream of mark-of-the-beast malarkey, and ridiculous claims which have lulled people to sleep rather than awakening them to the urgent signs of these perilous times.

It is crucial to understand that the decision to take the mark of the beast involves some form of a pledge of allegiance to the antichrist, making it a spiritual decision that has only secondary economic benefits. To receive the mark of the beast, citizens of the new world order will first have to pledge their unflagging support for the antichrist. This pledge of allegiance will mean they accept the beast's system of government, of finance, and of religion. It will mean that they buy into his vision, his platform, and his program.

From the Scriptures we know quite a bit about that program. Revelation 13 describes the beast's rise onto the world scene in some detail. It is an incredible overview of the last days system. Specifically, it tells us that when the beast rises onto the world scene, his first speeches and overtures to the world community will stress his hatred for God and all those who believe in Him.

> And there was given unto him a mouth speaking great things and blasphemies; and power was given unto him to continue forty and two months. And he opened his mouth in blasphemy against God, to blaspheme his name, and his tabernacle, and them that dwell in heaven. And it was given unto him to make war with the saints, and to overcome them: and power was given him over all kindreds, and tongues, and nations (verses 5-7).

Will the world accept this tirade of hate? Amazingly, not only will the people accept it, they will worship both the beast who speaks these words and also the devil himself!

> And they worshipped the dragon which gave power unto the beast: and they worshipped the beast, saying, Who is like unto the beast? who is able to make war with him? . . . And all that dwell upon the earth shall worship him, whose names are not written in the book of life of the Lamb slain from the foundation of the world (Revelation 13:4,8).

If we can understand the incredible nature of what will take place according to Scripture, then we can better understand the mark of the beast itself.

Don't forget that the mark of the beast is a sign of his followers' agreement with his opinion about God!

Taking the mark of the beast will not be some inadvertent act that will cost your very soul. People will know exactly what it means when they choose to accept it.

As antichrist speaks blasphemies against the one true God, his supporters will join in the chorus of railings and profanities toward their Creator. It is this action—combined with their attempts to create the "kingdom of man" in which God has no part—that constitutes an eternal, spiritual decision.

A Solemn and Eternal Warning

In this context, the Lord's solemn and eternal warning to those who would take the mark of the beast becomes completely understandable.

> If any man worship the beast and his image, and receive his mark in his fore-head or in his hand, the same shall drink of the wine of the wrath of God, which is poured out without mixture.... And the smoke of their torment ascendeth up for

ever and ever; and they have no rest day
or night, who worship the beast and his
image, and whosoever receiveth the mark
of his name (Revelation 14:9-11).

Certainly God would not pour out such awful
wrath upon anyone for purely economic reasons.
God would not condemn people to eternal punishment in hell just because they chose Visa over MasterCard, a smart card over a magnetic stripe card, or
some similar innocuous decision. Taking the mark
of the beast will not be some inadvertent act that will
cost your very soul. People will know exactly what it
means when they choose to accept it: making a
spiritual decision to serve the antichrist and worship the beast and his image. Verse 9 puts things in
their proper perspective: "If any man worship the
beast and his image, and receive his mark..." Note
carefully that worship of the beast precedes the
acceptance of the mark.

The Mark Is Given to Those Who Submit

The acceptance of the mark of the beast is a
result of personal, spiritual submission to the beast
himself. A conscious decision must be made to follow the antichrist. Only by pledging unswerving
devotion to the beast and his policies—economic,
political, and religious—will a person be allowed to
take the mark of the beast. Please take note of our
choice of words. Followers of the beast will be
allowed to receive this seal of approval. It will not
be forced on anyone. Only those who want it will
receive it.

They will want it not only so they can buy and sell, but because they have said (at least in their hearts), "We believe in this man. We believe he has the solutions for the problems that beset us. We believe that through the elimination of outdated religious ideas and nationalistic economic policies, this man can bring us peace and prosperity. We believe he is a god."

If you carefully study Revelation 13, you will see that the religious, political, and economic components of this new world order are so interconnected as to be inseparable. They work together to assure that you are either in or out of the system.

Since we have not yet taken the time to study the overall scope of Revelation 13—the chapter where the prophecy of the mark of the beast is found—let's do so now. Please read these verses carefully and prayerfully so that you can get a real sense of this soon coming new world order:

> And they worshipped the dragon which gave power unto the beast: and they worshipped the beast, saying, Who is like unto the beast? who is able to make war with him? And there was given unto him a mouth speaking great things and blasphemies; and power was given unto him to continue forty and two months. And he opened his mouth in blasphemy against God, to blaspheme his name, and his tabernacle, and them that dwell in heaven. And it was given unto him to make war with the saints, and to overcome them: and

power was given him over all kindreds, and tongues, and nations. And all that dwell upon the earth shall worship him, whose names are not written in the book of life of the Lamb slain from the foundation of the world. . . .

And I beheld another beast coming up out of the earth; and he had two horns like a lamb, and he spake as a dragon. And he exerciseth all the power of the first beast before him, and causeth the earth and them which dwell therein to worship the first beast whose deadly wound was healed. And he doeth great wonders, so that he maketh fire come down from heaven on the earth in the sight of men, and deceiveth them that dwell on the earth by the means of those miracles which he had power to do in the sight of the beast; saying to them that dwell on the earth, that they should make an image to the beast, which had the wound by a sword, and did live. And he had power to give life unto the image of the beast, that the image of the beast should both speak, and cause that as many as would not worship the image of the beast should be killed. And he causeth all, both small and great, rich and poor, free and bond, to receive a mark in their right hand, or in their foreheads: And that no man might buy or sell, save he that had the mark or the name of the beast, or the number of his name. Here is wisdom. Let him that hath understanding count the number of the beast: for it is the number of a man; and his number is Six hundred threescore and six (Revelation 13:4-18).

The Great Pretenders

Revelation 13:16,17 explains the economic ramifications of the beast's system. Revelation 13:4-8 demonstrates the breadth of antichrist's political control, and verses 11-15 show us the spiritual aspects of the new world order under antichrist.

Indeed, in these verses detailing the spiritual foundation of the beast's system, the third member of the unholy trinity is revealed. This hellish trinity is a counterfeit of the eternal trinity of the Father, Son, and Holy Spirit. Satan (or the dragon) represents the Father, while the first beast (the antichrist) is the counterpart of Jesus, the Son. Now we are introduced to the second beast, or the false prophet as he is called in Revelation 19:20, who is the counterfeit of the Holy Spirit.

Just as the Holy Spirit draws men to Christ and leads believers into the true worship of Jesus, this false prophet causes all to worship the beast (Revelation 13:12). Through impressive miracles, this second beast deceives those who remain upon the earth (verse 13).

Spiritual allegiance will be demanded. There will be no room for any other belief. Those who bow to the beast willingly and cheerfully commit their lives to the cause of the beast. They will be in total agreement with his political goals and plans, his economic program and his spiritual teachings. For this commitment, antichrist will mark them with his name or his number so that they can function in his new world order. They will joyously join the beast in blaspheming the one true God and revel in the killing of His followers. The age-old rebellion of man against God will reach its zenith in this unparalleled time of wickedness.

How Will Antichrist Do It?

We've often wondered how the antichrist could convince millions of people to receive his mark or his number when it has been so clearly and historically documented by Christians and unbelievers alike as an evil sign—a death knell. Anyone who has seen the movie *The Omen* knows that 666 is the number of the beast. Anyone who has read the Bible must know the number of the beast. Anyone with even a passing interest in rock music must have at least some knowledge of this prophecy.

How then will the antichrist convince so many people, who are so aware in some way of the mark and the number of the prophesied man of perdition, to receive just such a mark? Surely he would be clever enough to use 665 or any other number besides 666.

One possible scenario: The antichrist is openly speaking blasphemies against God, His Word, and His tabernacle. He is the pinnacle of arrogance in his supposed miraculous demonstrations and his contempt for holy things. He could try to use these "assets" to snare people into accepting the following line of thinking.

The antichrist could tell them they have been deceived and in bondage for too long to religious mythology and negative, intolerant traditions. Listen to this hypothetical, but very possible argument:

> We can no longer tolerate such narrow-minded and superstitious thinking in our new world of peace and harmony. We must all come together and demonstrate the success of our new world. We must not be paralyzed by superstitions and kept from the next step in our spiritual evolution. To prove we are not frightened by these "old wives' tales," we'll openly accept the challenge of failed Christianity and take for ourselves and our new world order the very symbol that these religious fanatics have erroneously associated with something sinister. We'll take 666 as our own!

We realize some readers will think we're being a little naive or simplistic here, but remember, those who have chosen to follow the beast will have made a fatal and eternal error. Following after the beast and taking his mark will ultimately damn their souls. The apostle Paul warned of this sad day almost 2,000 years ago:

> Even him [antichrist], whose coming is after the working of Satan with all power

and signs and lying wonders. And with all deceivableness of unrighteousness in them that perish; because they [antichrist's followers] received not the love of the truth, that they might be saved. And for this cause God shall send them strong delusion, that they should believe a lie: that they all might be damned who believed not the truth but had pleasure in unrighteousness (2 Thessalonians 2:9-12).

666: Man Becomes God

Many prophecy teachers have speculated concerning 666, the number of the beast. We have to be very careful here because such speculation has led to grave error. One thing we do know is that the number six in Bible numerology is considered to be the number of man. Three is considered to be one of the numbers of perfection, representing God. Thus, three sixes would indicate man's attempt to become God. This is the power and the strength of the beast's system, because the antichrist will brilliantly use man's pride to enslave him.

The antichrist will not only claim to be God, he will also claim that all people can attain godhood if they can just discover the divinity lying within them. It's the oldest lie in the book, but it has a remarkable history of success. You will recall that this was the very lie that deceived Lucifer when he fell from heaven:

How art thou fallen from heaven, O Lucifer, son of the morning! how art thou cut down to the ground, which didst weaken the nations! For thou hast said in thine heart, I will ascend into the heaven, I will exalt my throne above the stars of God: I will sit also upon the mount of the congregation, in the sides of the north: I will ascend above the heights of the clouds; I will be like the most High (Isaiah 14:12-14).

The lie that we can be gods is the same one that tripped up Eve in the garden of Eden:

And the serpent said unto the woman, Ye shall not surely die: For God doth know that in the day ye eat thereof, then your eyes shall be opened, and *ye shall be as gods*, knowing good and evil (Genesis 3:4,5).

The Real Armageddon

A positive proof of the nature of this new world order is found at the battle of Armageddon. Here all the nations of the earth are gathered to try to finish what Adolf Hitler started. They want to wipe the Jewish people off the face of the earth.

Why? Because Israel is the last remaining visible, recognizable, and attackable symbol of God in the world. Since this happens at the end of the seven-year period generally known as the Tribulation and since the church (made up of all believers in Jesus Christ) was raptured at the beginning of this period, the world has nowhere else to turn with its rage and hatred against anything connected to God!

Behold, I will make Jerusalem a cup of trembling unto all the people round about, when they shall be in the siege both against Judah and against Jerusalem. And in that day will I make Jerusalem a burdensome stone for all people . . . though all the people of the earth be gathered together against it. . . . And it shall come to pass in that day, that I will seek to destroy all the nations that come against Jerusalem (Zechariah 12:2,3,9).

And I saw three unclean spirits like frogs come out of the mouth of the dragon, and out of the mouth of the beast, and out of the mouth of the false prophet. For they are the spirits of devils, working miracles, which go forth unto the kings of the earth and of the whole world, to gather them to the battle of that great day of God Almighty. Behold I come as a thief. Blessed is he that watcheth, and keepeth his garments, lest he walk naked, and they see his shame. And he gathered them together into a place called in the Hebrew tongue Armageddon (Revelation 16:13-16).

Here is where the real unity of the new world becomes unquestionable. The spirit of antichrist and all those who follow him want only to destroy all things connected to the Lord. That is the unity of the antichrist order! This is when the Lord has had enough. This is when mankind as a whole, in perfect unison, has made its decision for the beast and his system.

> Then shall the Lord go forth, and fight against those nations, as when he fought in the day of battle (Zechariah 14:3).

> And I saw heaven opened, and behold a white horse; and he that sat upon him was called Faithful and True, and in righteousness he doth judge and make war. His eyes were as a flame of fire, and on his head were many crowns; and he had a name written, that no man knew, but he himself. And he was clothed with a vesture dipped in blood: and his name is called The Word of God. And the armies which were in heaven followed him upon white horses, clothed in fine linen, white and clean (Revelation 19:11-14).

What an incredible series of events we are talking about here! But we still haven't gotten to the most revealing part. At that time there will be no atheist or agnostic. No one will question the existence of God or hypothesize that God is dead. He will be right there. Every eye shall see Him!

Yet, will the world recognize its mistake or lack of faith? Will anyone say, "Oh, God, forgive my doubt" as did doubting Thomas when he finally saw the Lord? No. Rebellion, not repentance, will be the order of the day.

The evil of their hearts will be set, their determination so firm, that the entire world will unite as one behind the beast and try to blow the Lord out of the air. No further proof will be needed that this entire new order is born directly out of the rebellion that lies in man's heart.

> And I saw the beast, and the kings of the earth, and their armies, gathered together to make war against him that sat on the horse, and against his army (Revelation 19:19).

Of course, the Lord defeats His enemies with nothing more than a word out of His mouth, but the point is too important to miss. The new world order and the mark of the beast are the united world's statement that they do not want, need, or have any interest in God.

But let's not put this whole discussion in the future! For the same decision that the world faces tomorrow, we as individuals face today.

9

‖‖‖

The Chosen
Generation

Not long ago we saw a cartoon in a secular magazine. Two portly, middle-aged Wall Street types are walking down the street when they see the stereotypical doomsday prophet. You know the type: ankle-length robe, shoulder-length hair, scraggly beard, carrying a placard that reads "The End Is Near." One of the businessmen, his face betraying his fear, says to the other, "You know, he may be onto something."

There was also a recent special issue of *Time* magazine that discussed what it called "millennial fever," or the sudden interest in the future of mankind, the return of Christ, and other futuristic subjects. The *Time* authors said that such anxiety heightens at the beginning of each century, but takes on mammoth proportions during the transition from one millennium to another[1] (which makes us wonder: On what basis can they make such a claim, considering that we are only now completing the second millennium since Christ's first advent?).

Last Days Mockers

Despite increased interest in futuristic topics, there are only a few who think that Bible prophecy sheds much light on the current world situation. Mockers have said, "We've heard all this second-coming nonsense before. It's a fairy tale. Every generation for 2,000 years has said it would happen during their time, but nothing has happened yet."

You can hardly blame them. In the last half century, dozens of "antichrists" have come and gone—such as Mussolini, Hitler, Idi Amin, or more recently, Saddam Hussein. Christian fringe groups and non-Christian cults alike have set dates for the return of Christ that have long since come and gone. How can we forget the pandemonium that resulted from the unimpressive, but highly circulated *88 Reasons Why Jesus Could Return in 1988* and its even less impressive sequel—*89 Reasons*—the following year? More recently there was the Korean debacle (in which a huge church set a date for the rapture that subsequently passed uneventfully) that created economic and spiritual chaos for many, all because of faulty interpretations of Scripture and "new revelation." Each year there is an increasing number of books detailing not only the "time and season" but the "day and hour" of Christ's return. Maybe *Time* is right about apocalyptic fever!

In this light, maybe we have to admit that some of the declining interest in prophetic studies has been caused by prophecy teachers themselves! While trying to alert the world and the church to the imminent return of Christ, their good intentions often have been overshadowed by faulty methodology. If we may borrow from the comic strip character Pogo, "We have met the enemy and he is us."

Many startling fulfillments of Bible prophecy have occurred in recent years that clearly show this is probably the first generation fully capable of being the last.

Yet, those who scoff at the biblical prophecies are themselves a fulfillment of one such prophecy:

> Knowing this first, that there shall come in the last days scoffers, walking after their own lusts, and saying, Where is the promise of his coming? for since the fathers fell asleep, all things continue as they were from the beginning of the creation (2 Peter 3:3,4).

The Big Picture

And don't suppose that Peter's prophecy is the only one being fulfilled today! Many startling fulfillments of Bible prophecy have occurred in recent years (and they are still occurring as we write this book) that clearly show this is probably the first generation fully capable of being the last. Indeed, while virtually every generation has believed itself to be the prophesied last generation, we can point out a number of biblical prophecies that almost certainly could not have been fulfilled in any other generation.

Let's take a moment to consider the big picture. After all, there is such a thing as coincidence. Could the fulfillment of biblical prophecies be nothing more than an unlikely coincidence? Our answer is that God eliminated that possibility by giving us dozens of signs that would all come together in one final generation. This is where the proof lies.

So just to give you a sense of this big picture, let's stop for a moment and look at a few of the prophecies that are coming together in this generation.

Jews Return to Their Homeland

If there is one revelation at the center of Bible prophecy, it is the regathering of the Jews from the four corners of the earth to their own homeland. This was prophesied in many, many biblical passages. Allow us to reproduce just a few.

> I will take you from among the heathen, and gather you out of all countries,

and will bring you into your own land (Ezekiel 36:24).

It shall come to pass in that day, that the Lord shall set his hand again the second time to recover the remnant of his people, which shall be left.... And he shall set up an ensign for the nations, and shall assemble the outcasts of Israel, and gather together the dispersed of Judah from the four corners of the earth (Isaiah 11:11,12).

I will bring again the captivity of my people of Israel.... And I will plant them upon their land, and they shall no more be pulled up out of their land which I have given them, the LORD thy God saith (Amos 9:14,15).

The promise of these ancient prophecies started to become reality on May 14, 1948. The *New York Times* proclaimed the great fulfillment:

TEL AVIV, Palestine—The Jewish state, the world's newest sovereignty, to be known as the state of Israel, came into being in Palestine at midnight upon termination of the British mandate.[2]

A closely related development was the capturing by Israeli forces of the city of Jerusalem on June 7, 1967. In Luke 21:24, we read:

They shall fall by the edge of the sword, and shall be led away captive into all nations: and Jerusalem shall be trodden down of the Gentiles, *until the time of the Gentiles be fulfilled.*

The miracle that is Israel simply cannot be denied. After having been scattered to every nation of the earth, persecuted as no other people, and virtually wiped out by the Holocaust, the Jews today sit in their own land exactly as God promised.

> *The same generation that saw Israel reborn is also witnessing the European Community moving to the center of the world stage.*

But, prophetically speaking, that is not all. Israel is involved in the very peace process that ultimately will lead to the peace treaty of the antichrist. Jerusalem, a forgotten city for 2,000 years, is back at the center of world attention. Both Israelis and Palestinians claim her as their capital and she has indeed become a "burdensome stone," exactly as prophesied by the prophet Zechariah! And remember, none of this happened 1,000 years ago or 500 or even 200. *It happened in this very generation!*

A Geopolitical Textbook for the Nineties

Israel's return to her homeland is far from the only geopolitical development prophesied of the last days generation. Recall that the Roman Empire was a key player on the world scene in Jesus' time. Indeed, it was the Roman legions under Titus in A.D. 70 that destroyed Jerusalem and the temple, beginning 2,000 years of exile endured by the children of Abraham, Isaac, and Jacob. Four hundred years later, the Roman Empire itself vanished off the pages of world history.

But God told us that just as Israel would come back together in the last days, her great enemy would be revived as well. Today, the same generation that saw Israel reborn is also witnessing the European Community moving to the center of the world stage. No one in business will deny that this community will form the heart of the world's economy in the days ahead. No politician will deny that it is here that a new world order will find its base.

In that very generation—*this* generation—a military power unlike anything the world has ever known has formed to the north of Israel. And while many claim "the Soviet Union is dead," the fact is that the military might that made her one of the world's superpowers still exists. Some of its weapons has been dismantled, but dismantled is a far cry from destroyed!

The nations which comprised the Soviet Union and which today possess its weapons are far more unstable than the former superpower ever was.

And when you look at the makeup of the southern parts of the former empire, you realize they look a lot more like Iran than Russia. There could be just one target for all these weapons in the days ahead. And Israel knows it.

Exactly as prophesied in Ezekiel 38–39, a mammoth military machine sits to the north of Israel. Three of today's most prominent geopolitical powers were born in the same generation and all were prophesied as major, last days players. What are the odds of this being a mere coincidence?

The Beginning of Sorrows

One of the most frequent criticisms we hear about Bible prophecy is directed at Matthew 24:6-8, in which Jesus predicted that, just prior to His coming,

> [You will] hear of wars and rumours of wars . . . nation shall rise against nation, and kingdom against kingdom: and there will be famines, and pestilences, and earthquakes in divers places. All these are the beginning of sorrows.

Skeptics often reply that "there have always been earthquakes, famines, and pestilences. What makes this generation any different?"

We should first point out that when our Lord spoke of these calamities He referred to them as "the beginning of sorrows," or "birth pangs," as the original language has it. Thus, He was not saying that these things would take place only in the last days, but that like labor pains, they would become more intense and frequent in the last days.

Since this question is asked so frequently, however, let's focus on just two of these so-called general signs that Jesus told us would make up a part of the "beginning of sorrows"—earthquakes and pestilences.

Earthquakes Increasing

Jesus specifically told His disciples that in the last days there would be "earthquakes in divers places." Today, earthquakes are occurring in places like Egypt (December 1992), where an earthquake had never before been recorded. Moreover, earthquakes such as the recent one in Japan (July 1993) are increasing in frequency and magnitude. So great has this increase been that one dear lady painted a sign for our bus on a recent trip to Israel. She changed the name of our television broadcast from "This Week in Bible Prophecy" to "This Week in Earthquakes"! It seems as if we read of a major earthquake somewhere in the world every time we pick up the paper.

Of course, it is also true that seismic monitors now record earthquakes on the ocean floor and in remote mountain ranges. So skeptics sometimes claim, "Earthquakes aren't really increasing in number and magnitude. We just have better monitoring equipment today."

While this argument sounds perfectly reasonable, the fact is that when the earth shakes violently

Earthquakes 6.5 or Greater or Causing Significant Death or Damage		
1900–1969	48 earthquakes	*Average:* 6 per decade
1970–1989	33 earthquakes	*Average:* 17 per decade
Jan.–Jul. 1990	10 earthquakes	*Average:* 10 per 6 months
Jul. 1990–Oct. 1992	133 earthquakes	*Average:* 4.93 per month (600 per decade)

Source: Energy, Mines and Resources Canada

and buildings collapse and thousands of people are killed, you don't need sophisticated technology to tell you that you've had an earthquake!

Nevertheless, we decided to investigate the historical record of earthquakes. In order to make sure that we answered the skeptics' question of whether we are just better at detecting earthquakes today or if there really are more earthquakes occurring worldwide, we counted only major quakes.

According to the 1992 *Canadian Global Almanac*, 48 major quakes rocked the world between 1900 and 1969, averaging about six every ten years. Beginning in 1970, a new and alarming pattern began to develop. From 1970 to 1989, 33 major quakes shook various parts of the world, or about 17 per decade. In the first six months of 1990, ten major quakes killed more than 100,000 people. The frequency during this period increased from six rock-'em-sock-'em quakes every ten years to ten every six *months*.

So the question arises: Are the 1990 statistics a fluke, or are they evidence of a continuing pattern? We called Energy, Mines and Resources Canada, in Ottawa, the almanac's source, to find out. Bob North of the seismology department sent us a list of the major quakes since July of 1990. We asked him to use the same standards as were used to prepare the list for the almanac.

He listed significant earthquakes from July 1990 to October 12, 1992. (We know from news accounts that there have been many other major quakes since this report.) The list was ten pages long and showed that in just over two years, 133 major earthquakes have shaken the planet.

This isn't fiction or some stretch of the imagination. Jesus told us very clearly that earthquakes, like birth pangs, would increase in intensity and frequency in the last days. *And they are*. All we had to do was check out the facts.

AIDS and Other Pestilences

The second type of disaster Jesus mentioned in Matthew 24:7 was pestilences. Although they don't normally fall in the category of "natural disasters," the increase in disease and pestilence in recent years is a natural result of war and famine—two other evils Jesus mentioned in these same verses.

Increasingly we're hearing tragic reports that

diseases we thought had been eradicated are reappearing in more deadly strains. Polio, once thought to be eliminated by Dr. Jonas Salk's vaccine, has returned. Tuberculosis, once believed to be eliminated, is making a comeback. And penicillin and other antibiotics which used to be so effective in controlling disease are becoming increasingly impotent.

John Cionci, a medical doctor and a correspondent to "This Week in Bible Prophecy," has said that one of the main contributing factors to the increase of pestilence is space-age travel. Airliners turn epidemics into global pandemics.

Our global society has given us global exposure to once isolated problems. As more and more businesses and governments send representatives around the world, no country is immune to an outbreak of major plagues and diseases. Disease travels the world these days first class in jumbo jets.

We think it likely that AIDS is the worst plague in human history. It is estimated that the disease already has killed more than 152,000 persons in America alone.[3] In other parts of the world, particularly Africa and the Caribbean, the infection rate is pandemic. In Thailand, it has been found that 12 percent of all military inductees are HIV positive! Missionary sources tell us that in Uganda almost 50 percent of the population is infected with the HIV virus. A missionary acquaintance who pastors a large church there was told by government officials that he could expect to perform a dozen funerals a day for AIDS-stricken congregates in 1993.

The War to End All Wars

Another remarkable prophecy that seems to best fit this generation is also found in Matthew 24. In verse 22, Jesus described conditions just prior to His return: "And except those days should be shortened, there should no flesh be saved."

Jesus meant that if the days leading up to His second coming were not cut short, no man, woman, or child on the face of the earth would survive. Not one person hiding in a cave or living on an uncharted island or camping out in a remote forest would be left alive. If Jesus was referring to a destruction engineered by mankind, as His language seems to imply, then we must conclude that such universal devastation has never before been possible—that is, not until this present nuclear age.

Indeed, it wasn't that long ago that men battled with spears and bows and arrows. Even the major world wars were fought primarily with conventional weapons (considered primitive by today's standards). But this generation has seen the nuclear holocaust of Nagasaki and Hiroshima—and the weapons capability of the superpowers today makes those cataclysms seem almost trifling by comparison.

We are told that 50 percent of research scientists today are involved in arms development—and this in the "post-Cold War" age. Despite arms limitations talks and agreements, there is at least one military weapon and a corresponding 4,000 pounds of explosives for every man, woman, and child on the planet.

Until this generation, mankind simply did not possess such devastating power. Today, we indeed possess the ability to destroy all flesh . . . and the sad truth is that if God did not promise to intervene, we would do so!

And All the World Shall Wonder After the Beast

In the 18 short verses of Revelation 13, we are told of a global order featuring a world government, a world economy, a world military force, and even a world religion. Today, for the first time in history, we live in just such a "global community." Space travel and the mass media have altered the very fabric of our lives.

If the antichrist is to utterly dominate and lead the world, he must be able to communicate with that world. But instant, worldwide communication has not been possible in any generation before this one. Is it possible today? Just ask Madonna, Yasser Arafat, or Boris Yeltsin.

Unified Monetary System

Intrinsic to a global system is a global economy. Once again, this generation fits the bill. Harvard law professor Richard Cooper has suggested what he himself called a radical scheme:

> . . . the creation of a common currency for all of the industrial democracies, with a common monetary policy and a joint bank

of issue to determine that policy. . . . How can independent states accomplish that? They need to turn over the determination of monetary policy to a supranational body.[4]

In 1988, *The Economist* magazine announced the coming of a worldwide economy. The lengthy article, while noting that the international currency may be years away, did note that it "will be more convenient than today's national currencies, which will seem a quaint cause of much disruption to economic life in the twentieth century."[5]

The problem, according to the article, is that governments "are far from ready to subordinate their domestic objectives to the goal of international financial stability. Several more big exchange rate upsets, a few more stock market crashes and probably a slump or two will be needed before politicians are willing to face squarely up to that choice."[6]

Federal Reserve Chairman Alan Greenspan sees the future clearly, "I am very little concerned about the issue of foreign investment in the United States. On the contrary, integration of world economies is a desirable trend."[7]

World leaders are predicting and clamoring for a united economy, a centralized government, a single individual to lead mankind into the next millennium. These prophetic fulfillments surely sound an alarm to those who will hear. As our doomsday prophet at the opening of this chapter proclaimed, "The end is near." To deny such a reality is to stick your head in the sand and hope reality will go away.

When They Shall Say Peace and Safety

Are we the last generation? Speaking of the last generation, the Bible tells us in 1 Thessalonians 5:3:

> For when they shall say, Peace and safety; then sudden destruction cometh upon them, as travail upon a woman with child; and they shall not escape.

Paul received this revelation 2,000 years ago, and 500 years before that God had described the antichrist to His prophet Daniel: "By peace [he] shall destroy many" (Daniel 8:25).

Today, like during no other time in history, men and women around the globe are crying out for peace. Although wars continue to rage around the world, the major powers bask in a sense of peace. The Cold War is over. Nuclear holocaust, we are told, is a remote threat.

Even those who calculate the threat of nuclear war and the "end of the world" believe peace is here or very near. The Doomsday Clock was established in 1945 by atomic scientists to gauge the intensity of the Cold War and the likelihood of a nuclear exchange. It was closest to midnight—11:58—in 1953, after the United States tested the hydrogen bomb. At the close of the Cold War in 1992, these watchmen set the clock at 11:41—its furthest point from midnight since its inception.[8]

The New World Order

A broad spectrum of world leaders is calling for a coalition of nations to ensure the peace. Mikhail Gorbachev and George Bush brought the term "new world order" into our consciousness in their writings and speeches. Today, Bill Clinton, Boris Yeltsin, and Helmut Kohl promote the same vision. This new coalition is being formed to bring peace to the world—but men can never bring real peace. Man's efforts to play God will always fail. As admirable as the desire for peace and brotherhood is, it is also an impossibility when it is designed without the Prince of Peace at its foundation.

Today, like in the biblical times of the Tower of Babel (see Genesis 4:4-9), fallen man is trying to create a world in his image. He is trying to build a kingdom in which the wisdom of man is supreme and mankind itself is king. The ageless desire to control their own destiny is still with men today. But despite their boastful claims, their dream will never be fully realized. German Chancellor Helmut Kohl sees a day when . . .

> The United States of Europe will form the core of a peaceful order . . . the age prophesied of old, when all shall dwell secure and none shall make them afraid.[9]

The prophecy Kohl referred to describes the millennial reign of the King of kings and Lord of lords, but Kohl believes such a day can be created by man himself without the need of any Savior. And

Kohl is not alone. It seems this is an idea whose time has come.

> Just as the nation-state was a step in the evolution of the government at a time . . . we are now entering an era of new global interdependence requiring global systems of governance to manage the resulting conflicts . . . the growing tensions cannot be remedied by a single nation-state approach. They shall require the concerted effort of the whole world community.[10]

That was the heart of a pastoral letter from the National Conference of Catholic Bishops. Their prelate agrees. John Paul II says:

> The establishment of an order based on justice and peace is vitally needed today as a moral imperative valid for all peoples and regimes. . . . This is the only path possible.[11]

This desire for a global government transcends religious boundaries. Listen to the Rev. Franklyn Richardson of the Central Committee of the World Council of Churches:

> The World Council of Churches . . . I guess it's similar to the United Nations of the church. . . . I think that the future of the world is that we are becoming more of a village, that this is a global village. . . . We

are in one world, one community . . . the church is going to have to aid the world in understanding that and the United States is going to have to come to grips with that.[12]

When asked by *Time* magazine what mankind should aim to accomplish in the coming decades, a political scientist said:

> The central project of humanity has got to be something like restoration of a sense of community. . . . Giving up some individual rights to communities may be a necessary price. You cannot have the kind of culture that absolutizes human rights at the same time you strive for community. One has to come at the expense of the other.[13]

No matter how admirable the objectives of such a society, the actualization of such a system will be a frightening fulfillment of a major Bible prophecy. Yet the cries grow louder each day—as does the cry for a leader to show the way.

The World Leader

Chapter 13 of Revelation has been the focal chapter in our discussion of the mark-of-the-beast technology. Here, the seeming man of peace whom the Bible calls "the beast" is described in detail.

> All the world wondered after the beast . . . and they worshipped the beast, saying,

> Who is like unto the beast? who is able to make war with him? . . . And all that dwell upon the earth shall worship him, whose names are not written in the book of life of the Lamb (Revelation 13:3-8).

Although men have sought such a messianic personality for centuries, it has only been in this generation that serious men began to speak of the desperate need for such a global leader.

Walter Cronkite, probably the most respected news anchor in the industry even after his retirement, sums up the problem. He claims, "We exist in a leaderless world."[14] And historian Arnold Toynbee has written:

> By forcing on mankind more and more lethal weapons, and at the same time making the world more and more interdependent economically, technology has brought mankind to such a degree of distress that we are ripe for the deifying of any new Caesar who might succeed in giving the world unity and peace.[15]

But perhaps the most revealing call for a man of peace and power came from Henry Spaack, former secretary general of the North Atlantic Treaty Organization:

> What we want is a man of sufficient stature to hold the allegiance of all the people and to lift us out of the economic

morass into which we are sinking. Send us such a man and be he god or devil, we will receive him.[16]

Back to the Big Picture

The coming together of these prophecies in the same generation is something much more than a huge coincidence. All of these events seem to be working together to bring mankind toward events the Lord foretold long ago.

Calls for world peace, a new world order, a world economy, and even a world religion are beginning to dominate the news headlines. It all seems so logical—but what few realize is that the same logic for the same reasons once led to the building of something called the Tower of Babel.[17] Only today could it all happen on the global level predicted by Scripture. It was never before possible!

Imagine, If You Can

Perhaps a little mental exercise will help you to understand the magnitude of what we are talking about. Close your eyes and try to imagine what this world might be like in 2,000 years. What nation or nations will be ruling the world? Which disbanded nations will be regathered? What alliances will be in effect? What will be the state of national and international economies? Will there be peace? Will a major portion of the earth have been destroyed by earthquakes, nuclear war, or other man-made or natural disasters? What will life and society be like?

You just can't do it, can you? Neither can we. If you are like us, the only picture that comes to mind is George Jetson, his son Elroy, and their dog Astro.

The fact is that as rapidly as conditions are changing, it would be nearly impossible to answer these questions even if we were looking only *20* years into the future. The odds against accurately predicting just one event in the next 2,000 years is staggering.

But let's take it a step further. Imagine trying to predict an event that would occur during a specific generation during that 2,000-year span. The odds just took a quantum leap. Now, imagine predicting dozens of specific events, all coming together at the same time in that single generation. Now require that those dozens of events be the main focus of the front pages of that generation's newspapers (arms race, peace in Middle East, world economy, new world order, etc.).

You'll have to agree that it is unlikely that our finite minds could calculate the odds of even one successful prediction. The task of making scores of accurate predictions would be an utter impossibility . . . for man, that is. But all things are possible with God!

God predicted through His prophet Isaiah that He, and only He, could indeed do such a thing.

> Remember this, and shew yourselves men: bring it again to mind, O ye transgressors. Remember the former things of old: for I am God, and there is none else; I

am God, and there is none like me, declaring the end from the beginning, and from ancient times the things that are not yet done, saying, My counsel shall stand, and I will do all my pleasure.... Yea, I have spoken it, I will also bring it to pass; I have purposed it, I will also do it (Isaiah 46:8-11).

Bible prophecy is a tremendous affirmation that God is the one true God. No one but God would dare stake His reputation on foretelling the future. No other world religion includes prophecies in its sacred writings. Why not? Because religious systems designed by men cannot run the risk of having their spiritual house of cards demolished by the contrary winds of unfulfilled prophecies. Yet the one true God has precisely and unmistakably shown us the exact condition of the world just prior to the return of Christ.

The accuracy of Bible prophecy in foretelling these monumental events is phenomenal.

How can we doubt any longer that *this* generation is the first generation fully capable of being the last generation? And how can we still be skeptical of the One who told us of these things thousands of years ago?

The accuracy of Bible prophecy in foretelling these monumental twentieth-century events is phenomenal. Yet despite such precision, many ignore the warnings. At "This Week in Bible Prophecy," we believe that God has called us to document that the return of Christ is very near. This faith and this great hope are not built on a few random and isolated prophecies. It is not built on some farfetched interpretation that requires a vivid imagination to conceive. It is built simply on reading the Word of God and then looking at all of the major news events of our day. You don't need a handful of Ph.D.s to do that.

> For we have not followed cunningly devised fables, when we made known unto you the power and coming of our Lord Jesus Christ. . . . We have also a more sure word of prophecy; whereunto ye do well that ye take heed, as unto a light that shineth in a dark place, until the day dawn, and the day star arise in your hearts: Knowing this first, that no prophecy of the scripture is of any private interpretation. For the prophecy came not in old time by the will of man: but holy men of God spake as they were moved by the Holy Ghost (2 Peter 1:16,19-21).

A wise person knows enough to ignore a fable. But only the worst kind of fool chooses to disregard the truth. Which sort of person are you?

10

Where Will
You Stand?

Armageddon is coming. The day is fast approaching when the armies of the antichrist will stand as one to oppose the return of the Prince of Peace. Where will you stand in this battle to end all battles? Some might say they will make that decision when the battle begins. Others no doubt think we're crazy even to ask the question. Who in their right mind would choose to fight with the antichrist against God?

Yet millions are making just such a decision each day when they reject so great a salvation as that offered by God through His Son, Jesus Christ. For that is the heart of what Armageddon is all about. It is the world saying, "We will not bow our knee to anyone! We are too proud. We are too mighty. We are too important." This is the spirit of antichrist. It is also the opposite of the spirit of Christ:

> And being found in fashion as a man, he humbled himself, and became obedient unto death, even the death of the cross. Wherefore God also hath highly exalted him, and given him a name which is above every name: That at the name of Jesus every knee should bow, of things in heaven, and things in earth, and things under the earth; and that every tongue should confess that Jesus Christ is Lord, to the glory of God the Father (Philippians 2:8-11).

That is exactly what will happen. Despite their rebellion, the knee of every person at Armageddon shall indeed bow and the tongue of each shall indeed confess that Jesus Christ is Lord! But today the Lord seeks those who will confess Jesus as Lord and Savior *willingly*, recognizing their sin and the great love God has for them.

> For God so loved the world [mankind], that he gave his only begotten Son, that whosoever believeth in him shall not perish, but have everlasting life (John 3:16).

> That if thou shalt confess with thy mouth the Lord Jesus, and shalt believe in thine heart that God hath raised him from the dead, thou shalt be saved (Romans 10:9).

If we confess our sins, he is faithful and just to forgive us our sins, and to cleanse us from all unrighteousness (1 John 1:9).

Today Is the Day of Salvation

Today each of us faces his or her own personal Armageddon. We must choose which side we will be on. Those who reject God will grow closer and closer to a very subtle but real decision to join forces with the spirit of antichrist, blaspheme God, and fight against Christ in this hopeless battle. You are already on one of only two roads. There is no other option.

According to opinion polls, an overwhelming majority of North Americans believe they will spend eternity in heaven (about 93 to 95 percent). Yet it is obvious from the moral decay and decadence in the West that such a majority do not have the love of Christ in their hearts. Despite the claims of some preachers, the United States and Canada are not becoming more godly. In fact, just the opposite is true.

Many of those people who believe they are going to heaven apparently think they deserve to go because they were born in "Christian" nations or because their families have weddings and funerals in "Christian" churches, or because their ancestors were members of such churches. But none of these credentials will get a single person into heaven.

We must choose which side we will be on. Those who reject God will grow closer and closer to a very subtle but real decision to join forces with the spirit of antichrist.

Others point out that they are good people. They don't kick their neighbor's cat or cheat too much on their taxes. But none of this has any bearing on a person's eternal destiny. The Bible tells us clearly in the book of Romans that "all have sinned, and come short of the glory of God" (Romans 3:23). John tells us that if any man says he has not sinned, he is a liar (1 John 1:8,10).

No matter how good a person you are, you are still a sinner in the righteous eyes of God. You can never be good enough.

Imagine you were a great high jumper. You could have won an Olympic medal in the high jump. But no matter how talented you were, you couldn't jump to the moon.

That is a picture of how close our efforts at reaching God with our good works can come. No one can do it. But thank God, we don't have to!

The Price Has Been Paid

God knew we couldn't make it. The entire Old

Testament law was simply proof of how good you would have to be to make it to God by your own merits. The gulf of sin that separates us from God is just too great for us to cross.

That's why God paid the price for us. God sent His only begotten Son, Jesus, to pay the penalty for the sins of all mankind. Jesus, who knew no sin, became our sin offering. He offered His own life to God as a propitiation for our sins. He agreed to suffer the agony and indignity of Calvary's cruel cross to enable you and me to avoid eternal punishment and enjoy eternal life with Him.

> For God so loved the world [mankind], that he gave his only begotten Son, that whosoever believeth in him should not perish, but have everlasting life (John 3:16).

Jesus died for the sins of all mankind. You have only to realize that you are a sinner and need a Savior, and then accept the sacrifice that Jesus made for you. Those of us who have done just that are the "redeemed" of the Lord. Jesus, by His shed blood, has redeemed us, purchased us, bought us back for the Father. Because we have been reconciled to God, we are His children by adoption.

Right now, as you are reading this book, you can become one of the redeemed of the Lord. If you will admit you are a sinner, confess your sins, and ask God to forgive you based on the fact that Jesus already has paid the penalty for your sins, then God will forgive you. "If we confess our sins, he is faithful and just to forgive us" (1 John 1:9). The blood of

Jesus cleanses us from all unrighteousness. Your sins will be washed away by the blood of Christ.

Salvation is God's free gift. Forgiveness of sins is granted on the basis of God's grace and mercy. We can't earn forgiveness. No good works can save us. Yet *today* you can know forgiveness for your sins and freedom in Christ Jesus!

Why Not Come Home?

If that's your desire, I want you to pray the following prayer and be totally honest and sincere with God:

> Dear Father in heaven, I realize that I am a sinner and worthy of the fires of hell. At this moment, I confess my sins and ask You to forgive me for my rebellion against You and my refusal to accept the love of Christ. I accept the sacrifice that Your Son, Jesus, made for me on Calvary's cross. I believe that You raised Him from the dead, and I confess with my mouth that Jesus is my Lord. Thank You for hearing this prayer and accepting me into the family of God because of the blood of Christ that covers my sins. And I know from this moment on, I am saved. Thank You, Lord.

Those are simple words. There is nothing complicated about the gospel. In fact, the Bible tells us that the way is so simple that "wayfaring men, though fools [need] not err therein" (Isaiah 35:8). It isn't hard to understand the gospel. Nothing could be clearer:

> That if thou shalt confess with thy mouth the Lord Jesus, and shalt believe in thine heart that God hath raised him from the dead, thou shalt be saved (Romans 10:9).

But there is wise old saying to the effect that knowing what to do is not the problem—doing what we know is! It is just as true in the spiritual world. The Lord may have been dealing with you for a long time. But, like those poor souls at the battle of Armageddon, you have chosen to make war with the Lord instead of bowing before Him.

The hard part is not saying the words; it is saying them with all your heart. But do not fear, "For it is God which worketh in you *both* to will *and* to do of his good pleasure" (Philippians 2:13). God is for you. He is drawing you to Himself by His Spirit. He has a plan for you.

But you must decide. Choose this day whom you will serve!

The Bible tells us that the angels rejoice each time a sinner comes to Christ. We rejoice with you now if you made this most important decision in your life. We can only say, *"Welcome home!"*

Appendix

Check the Facts, Please

As we have stated many times in this book, the prophecy of the mark of the beast is one of the most important predictions in the entire Bible. This is so not only because the prophecy has become widely known in the secular world, but because it is so simple and clear.

The potential for its fulfillment in this generation is one of the most powerful witnessing tools we have. The enemy cannot change that fact—he can only try to discredit the message and surround the truth with so much false information that the truth gets lost. He also can try to get the discussion focused on secondary issues that mask the true meaning of the passage. Of course, he uses this tactic not only on prophetic passages, but on the entire Word of God. The Scripture tells us that we are not ignorant of the enemy's devices, and we must be very careful to avoid his trap of discrediting the Word of God.

But back to the main point. A failure to understand the spiritual significance of the mark of the beast has often led to an overemphasis on secondary economic issues. This, in turn, has resulted in a plethora of ridiculous rumors and silly superstitions.

In their eagerness to convince skeptics that this prophecy will soon come to pass, many prophecy buffs have often sensationalized the issues. This, unfortunately, has contributed to prophetic apathy rather than prophetic awareness.

And like all who spread unbiblical teachings and wild rumors, these sensationalists bring reproach upon the church and the Lord. Unfortunately, strange reactions to prophetic signs are not limited to the spiritually naive or immature. Even reputable Christian publications and media figures have often been caught up in these fantastic fantasies, perhaps because the time was not taken to check out details.

Many False Reports Abound

One excellent example of grist in the religious rumor mill comes from the early 1980s. Stories circulated throughout the North American church that the U.S. government had issued Social Security and other retirement checks on which was printed a restriction stating that the check could be cashed only if the bearer had a mark on his right hand or on his forehead.

As dramatic as this all sounded, we were amazed that not one of the hundreds of alleged recipients bothered to keep the check or at least photocopy it in order to prove the checks existed! To make matters worse, rumormongers reported that a red-faced government claimed the checks were issued prematurely and that the necessary identification system would not be in place until 1984 (the year of George Orwell's Big Brother). Despite a total lack of credible documentation, this bogus story was quickly reported by a number of Christian publications all over the continent.

The Computer Named "The Beast"

Then there was the tale of the giant computer called "The Beast," reportedly housed in Brussels, which was supposed to be keeping track of everyone in the world. The fact that no hard evidence of its capabilities was ever documented did not stop the sensationalists.

In yet another instance, it was reported that an entire town in Sweden had received the "mark of the beast" as a test for worldwide implementation. Another rumor suggested that high-security workers at a government installation in California were having microchips implanted under their skin for security purposes. In all these instances, proof was never given nor requested.

Throughout the years of "This Week in Bible Prophecy," we have made great efforts to document the possible fulfillments of prophecy. Documentation—that is the key. The prophecy of the mark of the beast does not need to be sensationalized. The fact that the technology and systems exist in the world today to make possible its fulfillment is sensational enough. False reports and silly rumors only damage the credibility of one of the most powerful prophetic passages in Scripture. We must be extremely careful about how we handle it.

An Element of Believability

Rumors like the foregoing often seem to possess a certain element of believability that make them easy to accept and to spread. Why? Perhaps because the source was supposedly a trustworthy Christian. Or perhaps it could be a case of the old tin can and string telephone game, where a sentence is whispered in the ear of each player and, by the time the sentence is repeated to its creator, it is seldom what it started out to be. Who knows where or how rumors start? The unfortunate thing is, sometimes they don't seem to stop.

Let's consider a couple of untrue stories that have made the Christian circuit for more than a decade. To this day we receive letters about these rumors, even though they were proven to be false years ago.

One widespread rumor involves Proctor & Gamble, the U.S. detergent and toothpaste maker. The rumor suggests that P&G is allegedly supporting the Satanist church. This tale also includes "confirmation" based on the supposed satanic symbolism of the 13 stars and the man-in-the-moon image that formerly adorned P&G packages. P&G finally got sick of the rumors and removed the symbol from their packaging.

There is no truth to either charge. The couple found to have originated the rumor were forced by a court of law to pay damages to P&G. Part of the P&G rumor is the story that a P&G executive appeared on a national television talk show, admitting the company's financial support of the Satanist church. In reality, no such interview ever took place.

Another fabrication involves the famed atheist, Madelyn Murray O'Hair and her alleged attempts to eliminate Christian programs from radio and television. The rumormongers tell us that she has petitioned the Federal Communications Commission to have such programming banned. To stop this archenemy of God, multiple thousands of believers have circulated petitions and mailed them to the FCC trying to stop O'Hair.

The truth is that there *was* a petition about 17 years ago that urged some changes in the procedures used by the FCC to regulate religious programming, but the petition—which was *not* initiated by O'Hair or her organization—was denied and the issue quickly laid to rest. Yet for the past decade and a half, dozens of bags of petitions continue to swamp FCC headquarters. Efforts have been made by almost every major Christian ministry to squelch this rumor, but it keeps resurfacing.

Rumors also have been spread that designer Liz Claiborne is a cultist. Claiborne has been confused by some with cult leader Elizabeth Clare Prophet, but the two are not the same.

These illustrations point out the power and the danger of rumors. They cause confusion and misdirect time and money from true kingdom work. These quixotic battles do great harm to the church. Similarly, such wild claims concerning the mark of the beast have contributed greatly to the apathetic attitude in the church about this key prophecy and others like it.

Superstitious Christians?

Superstition plays a big part in the mark-of-the-beast tales. Many otherwise solid believers would never write check number 666 for fear of damning their souls to eternal punishment. Others will skip over page 666 in a large book for fear some antichrist spirit would jump from the page and snare them. And yet other Christians refuse to have three consecutive sixes in their address or telephone number.

It needs to be emphasized that the number 666 occurs quite randomly and naturally in everyday life. And when it does, it has no hellish source or meaning. The number, of itself, is not evil. Coming into contact with it will not cause a person to be demonized.

People who like to play with numbers (known as numerologists) often try to identify evil entities by calculating the "number of his name." Using a simple system, these prognosticators have identified several persons, or things, as the antichrist.

One such system assigns a numerical value to each letter of the English alphabet (that restriction alone should invalidate any conclusion): *A* equals 6; *B* equals 12; *C* equals 18; etc. By using this system, numerologists have identified Adolf Hitler, Henry Kissinger, and the computer as the antichrist because the numerical value of their names totals the mystical 666.

As a matter of fact, under such a system Adolf Hitler actually totals 660, not 666, unless one uses a middle initial which would have to be an *A*. Kissinger fits only if you use his last name alone. The numerical value of the word *computer* is 666, but please don't try to convince your friends that the antichrist is a collection of circuits and chips and a motherboard.

Of course, there are a host of personal names and other nouns that total 666 using this system. Nevertheless, they have no negative connotations—much less a prophetic or satanic meaning.

Does any of this number-crunching prove anything? Of course not. It may seem like harmless fun, but there are prophecy buffs who spend hours doing such calculations to pinpoint dates, people, and events in Bible prophecy. Not only are such efforts a waste of time, they breed contention and confusion in the body of Christ.

There is little doubt that sensational stories and silly superstitions will increase as we draw nearer to the return of the Lord and a new millennium. Too, it is almost certain that there will be many Christians who, being "unskilful in the word of righteousness" (Hebrews 5:13), will help to spread these stories without making an attempt to verify them.

I beg you, don't be a part of the problem by spreading these rumors. Be part of the solution by checking out the rumors yourself and by requiring your sources to verify their facts. So-called prophecy ministries would be cut in half if we followed this simple advice.

Notes

Chapter 1—Boy, Have I Got Your Number
1. *Time* magazine, Nov. 11, 1991.
2. Ibid.
3. *L.A. Times*, July 1, 1986.
4. *Toronto Globe and Mail*, Aug. 14, 1993.
5. *National Notary*, Nov. 1993.
6. *Daily News*, Feb. 11, 1987.
7. *The Communicator*, Spring 1993.
8. *Washington Times*, Oct. 13, 1993.
9. Ibid.

Chapter 2—Kiss Your Cash Goodbye
1. US AIR Westbound Short Feature Reel, John Kramer, Nov. 6, 1993.
2. Danyl Corporation promotional literature.
3. Ibid.
4. Ibid.
5. Ibid.
6. Ibid.
7. Ibid.
8. Ibid.
9. Ibid.
10. Ibid.
11. Interviews at Solutions for Global Frontier Conference, Washington, D.C., Apr. 1993.
12. *Toronto Star*, Aug. 19, 1983.
13. Danyl Corporation.
14. George E. Word, *Time* magazine, Dec. 26, 1992.
15. *Journal Lorraine* newspaper, July 12, 1989.
16. *Philadelphia Inquirer*, Oct. 31, 1991.
17. Cedar Rapids *Gazette*, June 9, 1993.
18. Peter Lalonde, *One World Under Antichrist* (Eugene, OR: Harvest House Publishers, 1991), p. 236.

Chapter 3—What's in the Cards?
1. Sid Price, senior vice-president of National Processing Company, at the CardTech/SecurTech Conference.
2. *Christian World Report*, June/July 1992.
3. Ibid.
4. Sid Price, CardTech/SecurTech Conference.
5. *Card Technology Today*, Nov. 1992.
6. Ibid.
7. Ibid., Oct. 1992.
8. US AIR cinema, Nov. 6, 1993.
9. *Card Technology*, Nov. 1992.
10. *Smart Card Monthly*, Apr. 1993.
11. Ibid.
12. Cited in *SCIA Communicator*, Spring 1993.
13. *Card Technology*, Nov. 1992.
14. *This Week in Bible Prophecy* magazine, Vol. 1, Is. 2.
15. Ibid.
16. *U.S. News & World Report*, Dec. 17, 1984.
17. Federal Reserve Bank of Atlanta Economic Review, Mar. 1986.
18. Ibid.

Chapter 4—Your Body: The Only ID You'll Ever Need
1. *Automatic I.D. News*, June 1992.
2. Ibid.
3. Stephen Seidman, quoted in *Automatic I.D. News*, June 1992.
4. *PIN: Personal Identification News*, Mar. 1993.
5. Identix promotional literature.
6. *Herald Statesman*, Westchester County, June 7, 1989.
7. *International Herald Tribune*, Nov. 6, 1992.
8. *Card Technology Today*, July/Aug. 1992.
9. *Biometric Technology Today*, Apr. 1993.
10. From a paper presented by James Holmes of Sandia National Laboratories for the CardTech/SecurTech Conference, Washington, D.C., Apr. 1993.

11. *Biometric Technology,* Apr. 1993.
12. Solutions for Global Frontier Conference, Washington, D.C., Apr. 1993.
13. Cedar Rapids *Gazette,* Jan. 11, 1992.
14. *Biometric Technology,* Apr. 1993.

Chapter 5—Will That Be Hand or Forehead?
1. Gannett News Service, as quoted in the *Omega-Letter,* Oct. 1986.
2. Terry Galanoy, *Charge It* (New York: Putnam Publishers, 1980).
3. *Omega-Letter,* Mar. 1988.
4. *Buffalo News,* Mar. 19, 1991.
5. *Omega-Letter,* Mar. 1988.
6. Ibid.
7. *Omni,* Mar. 1987.
8. Peter Lalonde, *One World Under Antichrist* (Eugene, OR: Harvest House Publishers, 1991), p. 242.
9. Originally from Associated Press, July 19, 1987.
10. Gannett News, *Omega-Letter.*
11. *USA Today,* June 28, 1989.
12. Associated Press, July 19, 1987.
13. RMI Regional Marketing Inc. promotional literature.
14. Associated Press as quoted in the *Omega-Letter,* Mar. 1988.
15. *Cat Fancy* magazine, Oct. 1984.
16. *Toronto Star,* Dec. 16, 1991.
17. Ad in *American Biotechnology Laboratory,* June 1991.
18. Quoted in the *Omega-Letter,* Feb. 1987.
19. Oceanside *Blade Citizen,* Sep. 18, 1993.
20. *Allentown Morning Call,* July 10, 1993.
21. PETNET promotional literature.

Chapter 6—If You're Not Paranoid . . .
1. Toronto *Globe,* Aug. 14, 1993.
2. *National Notary,* Nov. 1993.
3. *USA Today,* Oct. 1, 1993.
4. Ibid.
5. *The European,* Feb. 6, 1992.
6. Midnight Call, May 1992.
7. Quoted in *St. Petersburg Times,* Sep. 23, 1992.
8. *The Economist,* Aug. 24, 1991.
9. Quoted in Cedar Rapids *Gazette,* Jan. 10, 1993.
10. Applied Systems Institute, Inc. promotional literature.
11. *Fairborne Daily Herald* (OH), Jan. 11, 1991.
12. *Union Leader,* Nov. 12, 1992.
13. *New York Times,* Aug. 18, 1991.
14. *Card Technology Today,* July/Aug. 1992.
15. Ibid.
16. *Sky Magazine,* Mar. 1991.
17. Ibid.
18. Ibid.
19. Ibid.
20. *Card Technology.*
21. *European,* July 30, 1992.
22. *Milwaukee Journal,* Oct. 11, 1992.
23. Associated Press, Sep. 27, 1987.
24. Terry Galanoy, *Charge It* (New York: Putnum Publishers, 1980).

Chapter 7—Bringing the World On-Line
1. *Omni* magazine, Dec. 1991.
2. Ibid.
3. Ibid.
4. *Time* magazine, Jan. 27, 1992.
5. Annual Report of Information Commission of Canada, 1990-91.
6. *Time,* June 24, 1991.
7. As reported in *Toronto Star,* Aug. 6, 1991.
8. Joseph Battaglia, quoted in *The McAlvany Intelligence Advisor,* July 1991.
9. Ibid.
10. *The McAlvany Intelligence Advisor,* July 1991.
11. Ibid.
12. *USA Today,* May 6, 1991.
13. *International Herald Tribune,* July 6, 1993.
14. *Time,* July 12, 1993.

15. "Borderless Borders: The First World Pragmatech Card Conference," Barcelona, Spain, Mar. 13-15, 1991.
16. Ibid.
17. *USA Today*, Apr. 21, 1993.

Chapter 9—The Chosen Generation
1. *Time* magazine, special edition, "Beyond the Year 2000," Fall 1992.
2. *New York Times*, May 15, 1948.
3. Associated Press, Oct. 28, 1992.
4. *Foreign Affairs* magazine, Fall 1984.
5. Cited in Peter Lalonde, *One World Under Antichrist* (Eugene, OR: Harvest House Publishers, 1991), p. 270.
6. Ibid.
7. Ibid.
8. Associated Press, Nov. 27, 1991.
9. Ibid., June 8, 1990.
10. Cited in J. Dwight Pentecost, *Things to Come* (Grand Rapids, MI: Zondervan, 1958).
11. Lalonde, *One World*, p. 269.
12. Ibid.
13. *Time*, "Beyond the Year 2000."
14. Lalonde, *One World*, p. 266.
15. Ibid.
16. Ibid., p. 267.
17. See Genesis 11:1-4. The key point here is that man was trying to come together "lest they be scattered abroad." The Hebrew here means "utterly destroyed." People today are trying to build a tower of peace so they won't be destroyed. Like the men of Babel who felt self-sufficient and did not need God to accomplish their purposes, modern man is trying to bring about through the "arm of flesh" that which can only be accomplished by the Prince of Peace when He returns in power and great glory. The plans and schemes of man, from Babel to the New Age movement, have not changed at all.

For More Information

If you are interested in knowing more about This Week in Bible Prophecy or any of the products listed on the following pages, please contact:

This Week in Bible Prophecy
P.O. Box 1440
Niagara Falls, NY 14302-1440

P.O. Box 665
Niagara Falls, ON L2E 6V5

1-905-684-7700

THE ORIGINAL!

The Mark of the Beast

The Mark of the Beast - it's one of the clearest and most dramatic prophecies in the Bible. It states simply that in the last days that no man will be able to buy or sell unless he has the mark IN his right hand or forehead.

Years ago such a thing would have been impossible. But now the technology exists. This video report, with Peter Lalonde, producer and co-host of the *This Week In Bible Prophecy* television program, will cut through all the stories and give you all the facts. From the development of the cashless society, to hand-scanners, and actual micro-chip implants - you will see the latest technology explained in one of the most dramatic prophetic videos ever produced.

"Whether they realize it or not, some of today's largest corporations are actually testing the Mark of the Beast."
- Peter Lalonde

Mark of the
Beast II

Join Peter and Paul Lalonde as they take an in depth and completely up-to-date look at one of the Bible's most fascinating prophecies. You'll see how quickly the technology needed to make this prophecy come to pass has raced along the road from impossible to likely, from probable to undeniable and finally to reality. Fascinating to both believers and skeptics alike, this video is sure to make a lot of people sit up and take notice of God's warnings about these last days.

It's like having a book on Bible prophecy that never ends. Always exciting and never out of date!

In every issue of *This Week In Bible Prophecy Magazine* we have feature reports on some of the most current fulfilments of Bible prophecy in this generation. From the *Mark of the Beast*, to the Middle East - from the New World Order, to the new age movement - you'll get all the facts in an exciting, easy-to-read format.

You'll also get all of the latest ministry updates, *"Behind the Scenes"* information, and the hopes and dreams of Peter, Patti and Paul Lalonde.

On the program, Peter and Paul show some of the most dramatic evidences of the fulfilment of prophecy that you could ever imagine. In this magazine these evidences are reproduced, in full colour, for your personal research and witnessing.

There is no question that Peter Lalonde has become one of the clearest and most trusted voices in Bible prophecy. Now, he will answer your questions about the Bible and its relevance to our day in our special *"Ask Peter"* section.

Patti Lalonde will keep you up-to-date on the most current events, opinions and influences of the mass media in the monthly section called, *"The Media Report"*.

Every month there are dozens of little tidbits of news and information that come into our offices. These are items that we know will fascinate the student of Bible prophecy, so we have expanded the *"Signs of the Times"* section. ■

"This Generation Shall Not Pass"
The Prophecies of Matthew 24

In this powerful new prophetic video, you'll join Peter and Paul Lalonde for an amazing 90 minute journey through the verses of the Olivet Discourse. You'll be amazed as you see just how clearly Jesus' prophecies are being fulfilled today. It's as if the disciples were given a glance at today's newspaper headlines.

Even the toughest skeptic can't argue with the facts contained in Matthew 24. It's very clear...Here is what the Bible says—and here is the evening news. Only God can save the soul of an unbeliever, but we can help to lead the way.

Become a prophecy expert in just days ...

30 Days to Bible Prophecy

A Step by Step Journey to Understanding Bible Prophecy

You are living in a world that witnesses first hand prophecies being fulfilled everyday. But what does this mean? When will you know its time for His arrival? Are you prepared for this day?

These and many more questions are answered with the *30 Days to Bible Prophecy* program. From the producers of *This Week In Bible Prophecy*, comes one of the most comprehensive prophetic educational programs available.

When you order *30 Days to Bible Prophecy* you'll recieve:

❖ 30 in-depth conversations with Peter and Paul Lalonde covering dozens of the most important prophetic themes found in the Bible.

❖ 5 full length Study Guides designed to help you to understand these last days

❖ 10 Special Reports

❖ *"Excitement of His Coming"* video - Peter Lalonde shares with you his own personal testimony, his interest in prophecy and the impact that prophecy has had on his own life

❖ Special video report on the New Age Movement prepared by 100 Huntley Street featuring Peter Lalonde

"Blessed is he that readeth, and they that hear the words of this prophecy, and keep those things that are written therein: for the time is at hand." Revelation 1:3

For more information, contact:

This Week in Bible Prophecy

| P.O. Box 1440 | P.O. Box 665 |
| Niagara Falls, NY 14302-1440 | Niagara Falls, ON L2E 6V5 |

1-905-684-7700